GCSE OCR Gateway
Additional Science
Higher Workbook

This book is for anyone doing
GCSE OCR Gateway Additional Science at higher level.

It's full of **tricky questions**... each one designed to make you **sweat**
— because that's the only way you'll get any **better**.

There are questions to see **what facts** you know. There are questions
to see how well you can **apply those facts**. And there are questions
to see what you know about **how science works**.

It's also got some daft bits in to try and make the whole
experience at least vaguely entertaining for you.

What CGP is all about

Our sole aim here at CGP is to produce the highest
quality books — carefully written, immaculately presented
and dangerously close to being funny.

Then we work our socks off to get them
out to you — at the cheapest possible prices.

Contents

MODULE B4 — IT'S A GREEN WORLD

MODULE C4 — CHEMICAL ECONOMICS

MODULE P4 — RADIATION FOR LIFE

Published by Coordination Group Publications Ltd.

Editors:
Ellen Bowness, Tom Cain, Sarah Hilton, Kate Houghton, Sharon Keeley, Andy Park,
Kate Redmond, Rachel Selway, Ami Snelling, Sarah Williams.

Contributors:
Michael Aicken, Tony Alldridge, Peter Cecil, Claire Charlton, Steve Coggins,
Vikki Cunningham, Jane Davies, Ian H Davis, Mike Dagless, Catherine Debley, Max Fishel,
James Foster, Andrew Furze, Giles Greenway, Anna-fe Guy, Dr Iona MJ Hamilton,
Derek Harvey, Rebecca Harvey, Frederick Langridge, Barbara Mascetti, Lucy Muncaster,
John Myers, Andy Rankin, Sidney Stringer Community School, Claire Stebbing,
Paul Warren, Chris Workman.

ISBN-10: 1 84146 742 1
ISBN-13: 978 1 84146 742 9

With thanks to Vanessa Aris, Barrie Crowther, Ian Francis and Glenn Rogers for the proofreading.
With thanks to Jan Nash and Katie Steele for the copyright research.

Diagram on page 22 from Roland Soper, Biological Science 2 (1985). By permission of
Cambridge University Press.

Data table on page 94 from Roland Soper, Nigel PO Green, G Wilfred Stout, Dennis J Taylor,
Biological Science Combined Volume Hardback (1990). By permission of Cambridge University Press.

Data used to construct pie chart on page 111 from "Concise Dictionary of Chemistry"
edited by Daintith, J (1986). By permission of Oxford University Press. www.oup.com

Groovy website: www.cgpbooks.co.uk

Printed by Elanders Hindson Ltd, Newcastle upon Tyne.
Jolly bits of clipart from CorelDRAW®

Cells and DNA

Q1   Complete each statement below by circling the correct words.

a)   Plant / Animal cells contain chloroplasts, but plant / animal cells don't.

b)   Plant cells have a vacuole / cell wall, which is made of cellulose.

c)   Both plant and animal cells / Only plant cells / Only animal cells contain mitochondria.

d)   Chloroplasts are where respiration / photosynthesis occurs, which makes glucose / water.

Q2   Choose from the words below to complete the passage about the **structure of DNA**.

| U | base | A | helix | cytoplasm |
| protein | G | nucleotides | B | nucleus |

DNA is found in the .... of most animal cells. It is a

double-stranded .... made up of lots of ....

Each nucleotide contains a small molecule called a ....

There are four of these — ...., C, ... and T.

Q3   **Mitochondria** are very important cellular structures.

a)   Is this cell an animal or plant cell? ....

b)   Draw an arrow pointing to a mitochondria in the cell.

c)   Why are mitochondria so important?

....

....

Q4   Complete the diagram below to show which **bases** will form the complementary strand of DNA.

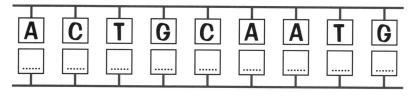

Q5   Number the statements below to show the correct order of the stages in **DNA replication**.

☐   Cross links form between the bases of the nucleotides and the old DNA strands.

☐   The DNA double helix 'unzips' to form two single strands.

☐   The result is two molecules of DNA identical to the original molecule of DNA.

☐   Bases on free-floating nucleotides pair up with matching bases on the DNA strand.

☐   The new nucleotides are joined together, to make new strands of DNA.

DNA Fingerprinting

Q1   Choose the correct word to complete each of the following sentences about DNA fingerprinting.

a)   DNA molecules have a **negative** / **positive** electric charge.

b)   Before DNA fingerprinting can start, the DNA must be **isolated** / **replicated**.

c)   The DNA sample is broken down into fragments using **acids** / **enzymes**.

d)   DNA fragments are separated using **electric current** / **photographic film**.

e)   Larger DNA fragments **move further than** / **don't move as far as** smaller DNA fragments.

f)   DNA can be made to show up on photographic film if it is marked by **radioactivity** / **staining**.

Q2   Choose from the words below to complete the passage about the **DNA fingerprinting** process.

| positive | negatively | bigger | chromatography |
| smaller | positively | suspended | negative | separated |

After the DNA has been cut into fragments, these fragments are ....

using a process a bit like .... They're .... in a gel,

and an electric current is passed through the gel. DNA is .... charged,

so it moves towards the .... anode. .... bits travel faster

than .... bits, so they move further through the gel.

Q3   The following **DNA samples** are being used in a **murder investigation**. The DNA samples are from the victim, three suspects and some blood which was found on the victim's shirt.

a)   Which two individuals are likely to be **related** to each other? Explain your choice.

....

....

Victim   Blood found   Suspect A   Suspect B   Suspect C
on shirt

b)   Who is the most likely culprit based on the DNA evidence? Explain your answer.

....

c)   Can this suspect be accused of murder beyond all doubt? Explain your answer.

....

....

Module B3 — Living and Growing

DNA Fingerprinting

Q4 **Genetic fingerprinting** is a way of comparing people's DNA — it's useful in forensic science. Put the following stages of DNA fingerprinting into the correct order.

Compare the unique patterns of DNA.

Separate the sections of DNA.

Isolate the DNA from the cells.

Cut the DNA into small sections.

1. ....

2. ....

3. ....

4. ....

Q5 A thoroughbred horse breeder has collected DNA samples from each of her horses. Her **new foal's DNA** is **sample 1**. The **mother** of the foal is **sample 2**. Study the **DNA profiles** and complete the table showing which horse is the **foal's father**.

Sample 1 (foal)   Sample 2 (mother)   Sample 3 (male)   Sample 4 (male)   Sample 5 (male)

	Foal	Mother	Father
DNA sample	Sample 1	Sample 2	

Q6 A national **genetic database** would allow everyone's unique pattern of DNA to be saved on file.

a) Give one use of a national genetic database.

....

b) Give one drawback of a national genetic database.

....

Protein Synthesis and Enzymes

Q1 a) Tick the boxes to show whether the sentences are **true** or **false**.

       True False

  i) Most enzymes are made of fat. ☐ ☐

  ii) The rate of most chemical reactions can be increased by increasing the temperature. ☐ ☐

  iii) Most cells are damaged at very high temperatures. ☐ ☐

  iv) Each enzyme can speed up a lot of different reactions. ☐ ☐

b) Write a correct version of each false sentence in the space below.

....

....

Q2 Circle the correct words below to complete the sentences.

a) Proteins are made up of chains of amino acids / glucose.

b) Transamination happens in the kidneys / liver.

c) Each amino acid is coded for by a sequence of three / four bases.

Q3 Draw lines to match each of the terms below with its correct description.

amino acid   a biological catalyst

DNA   a molecule containing many genes

enzyme   a section of DNA that codes for a protein

gene   a molecule that is coded for by a gene

protein   a building block for a protein

Q4 DNA controls the production of **proteins**.

a) How do **amino acids** determine the function of a protein?

....

b) What happens if we don't take in the full range of amino acids in our **diet**?

....

c) Explain the role of the **bases** in DNA in the building of a protein.

....

....

Enzymes

Q1 Enzymes are essential for many life processes.

a) Write a definition of the word '**enzyme**'. ....

....

b) Draw a sketch in the space
on the right to show how an
enzyme's shape allows it to
break a substance down.

Q2 This graph shows the results from an investigation into the effect
of **temperature** on the rate of an **enzyme** catalysed reaction.

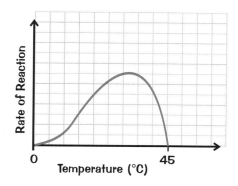

a) What is the **optimum** temperature for this enzyme?

....

b) Describe what happens to the structure of an enzyme at
temperatures **above** its optimum.

....

....

Q3 **Catalase** is an enzyme found in potatoes. It catalyses the following reaction:

hydrogen peroxide → oxygen + water

Julianna is investigating the effect of **temperature** on
catalase. She cuts up a potato, adds the pieces to a
test tube containing hydrogen peroxide and measures
the amount of oxygen produced using the apparatus
in the diagram. She repeats the experiment using
different temperatures.

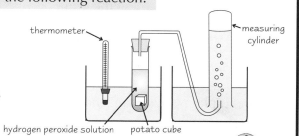

a) i) What is the **independent** variable? ....

ii) What is the **dependent** variable? ....

b) The first time Julianna tried this experiment, the reaction was very slow.
Suggest how she could increase the reaction rate (except by increasing the temperature).

....

c) Give two ways Julianna can help make it a fair experiment.

....

....

Enzymes

Q4   Draw lines to match the words below about **enzyme action** with their meanings.

active site

denaturing

optimum

specificity

substrate

the best conditions for enzyme action

the chemical substance that an enzyme works on

destroying an enzyme by exposing it to the wrong conditions

the idea that enzymes only work with one substrate

the part of an enzyme which the substrate attaches to

Q5   Stuart has a sample of an enzyme and he is trying to find out what its **optimum pH** is. Stuart tests the enzyme by **timing** how long it takes to break down a substance at different pH levels. The results of Stuart's experiment are shown in the table below.

pH	time taken for reaction in seconds
2	101
4	83
6	17
8	76
10	99
12	102

a)   Draw a line graph of the results of the experiment on the grid opposite.

b)   What is the **optimum** pH for the enzyme?

    ....

c)   Explain why the reaction is very slow at certain pH levels.

    ....

d)   Would you expect to find this enzyme in the stomach? Explain your answer.

    ....

e)   Describe **two** things that Stuart would need to do to make sure his experiment is a fair test.

    1. ....

    2. ....

Top Tips: Enzymes crop up a lot in Biology so it's worth spending plenty of time making sure you know all the basics. If you're finding things a bit dull, you could always take a little break and eat some tofu to make sure you have enough protein to make lots of delightful enzymes.

Diffusion

Q1 Complete the passage below by choosing the most appropriate words.

Diffusion is the **direct** / **random** movement of particles from an area where they are at a **higher** / **lower** concentration to an area where they are at a **higher** / **lower** concentration. The rate of diffusion is faster when the concentration gradient is **bigger** / **smaller** and in **liquids** / **gases**. It is slower when there is a **large** / **small** distance over which diffusion occurs and when there is **more** / **less** surface area for diffusion to take place across.

Q2 The first diagram below shows a **cup of water** which has just had a **drop of dye** added.

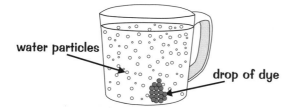 

a) In the second cup above, draw the molecules of **dye** in the water after an hour.

b) Predict how the rate of diffusion of the dye would change in each of the following situations:

   i) a large drop of dye is used rather than a small drop of dye

   ....

   ii) the water is heated

   ....

   iii) the dye and water are placed in a long thin tube

   ....

c) Explain the movement of the dye particles in terms of differences in concentration.

....

....

Q3 Patsy was studying in her bedroom. Her dad was cooking curry for tea in the kitchen. Soon Patsy could smell the curry that her dad was making.

a) Her dad was warm so he switched on a fan. Suggest what effect the fan would have on the rate that the curry particles spread through the house.

....

b) After tasting the curry, Patsy's dad added more curry powder. What effect would this have on the smell of the curry? Explain your answer using the word **concentration**.

....

....

Diffusion

Q4 Some statements about **diffusion** are written below.
Decide which are correct and then write **true** or **false** in the spaces.

a) Diffusion takes place in all types of substances. ....

b) Diffusion is usually quicker in liquids than in gases. ....

c) Diffusion happens more quickly when there is a higher concentration gradient. ....

d) A larger surface area makes diffusion happen more quickly. ....

e) When there is a larger distance for particles to travel across, the rate of diffusion is faster. ....

Q5 Two diagrams of diffusion are shown below.

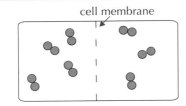

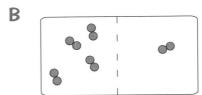

Would you expect the molecules to diffuse **faster** in situation A or B? Explain your answer.

....

....

Q6 Phil was investigating the diffusion of **glucose** and **starch** through a **membrane**.
He placed equal amounts of glucose solution and starch solution inside a bag
designed to act like a cell membrane. He then put the bag into a beaker of water.

a) After an hour, Phil tested the water for the presence
of starch and glucose. Circle which of the following you
would expect to be found in the water outside the bag:

glucose   starch

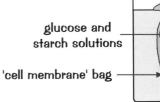
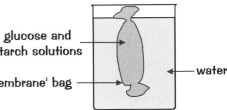

b) Explain your answer to part a).

....

....

c) Phil did the experiment again using the same amounts of glucose
and starch solutions. This time he used a much longer, thinner bag.

Will the diffusion happen faster or more slowly this time?
Explain your answer.

Think about the surface areas of the bags.

....

....

Top Tips: Don't forget — it's only small molecules that can diffuse through cell membranes, e.g. glucose, amino acids, water and oxygen. Big hulking things like proteins and starch can't fit through.

Module B3 — Living and Growing

Diffusion in Cells

Q1 Tick the boxes to show whether the statements below are **true** or **false**.

True False

a) Diffusion is the movement of particles from an area of higher concentration to an area of lower concentration. ☐ ☐

b) In the placenta, the mother's blood mixes with the foetus's blood. ☐ ☐

c) Villi are present in both the placenta and the small intestine. ☐ ☐

d) The alveoli and the placenta both have a good blood supply. ☐ ☐

e) The foetus absorbs oxygen from the mother's blood in the umbilical cord. ☐ ☐

f) The surface of the alveoli is moist. ☐ ☐

g) To pass on a nerve impulse, a transmitter substance diffuses across a synapse. ☐ ☐

Q2 Circle the correct words to complete the paragraph below.

Proteins in our food are digested to produce **amino acids / starch**. This makes the molecules **large / small** enough to enter the bloodstream by **diffusion / osmosis**. This happens because their concentration in the blood is **higher / lower** than in the gut. Later, when the blood reaches the cells in the body that are using up the food substances, the food molecules move **into / out of** the bloodstream.

Q3 Use the words below to complete the passage about transmission between nerve cells.

impulse   binds   digestive   diffuses   nerve
dove   membrane   receptor   synapse   lapse   transmitter

The gap between one .... cell and the next is called a .... When a nerve .... arrives, it causes the release of a .... substance from the first nerve cell. This .... across the gap, and .... to a .... in the end of the next cell.

Q4 Oxygen diffuses into the blood through the walls of the **alveoli**.

a) Describe **two** ways in which the structure of the alveoli helps efficient diffusion.

....

....

b) What effect would holding your breath have on the rate of absorption of oxygen?

....

Diffusion in Cells

Q5   The diagram below shows an **alveolus** and a **capillary**.

a) On the diagram, label the **alveolus**, a **red blood cell** and a **capillary wall**.

b) Air is being breathed **into** the lungs. On the diagram:

   i) draw an arrow to show the movement of air molecules due to breathing. Label this arrow **X**.

   ii) draw an arrow to show the diffusion of oxygen molecules. Label this arrow **Y**.

   iii) label with the letter **Z** the red blood cell which has the lowest oxygen concentration.

c) As a person breathes **out**, is oxygen diffusing into or out of the blood? Explain your answer.

....

....

d) Describe the movement of carbon dioxide from inside a body cell to outside the body via the blood. Use the terms, **higher concentration**, **lower concentration** and **diffuse**.

....

....

....

....

Q6   The **placenta** connects the mum and baby when a mammal is pregnant.

a) Describe, in terms of areas of higher and lower concentrations, how:

   i) food and oxygen reach the foetus.

....

....

   ii) carbon dioxide and other waste substances are removed through the placenta.

....

....

b) Explain how the placenta is adapted to increase the rate of diffusion.

....

....

Diffusion in Cells

Q7 The **small intestine** is adapted for the absorption of food.

a) Label the diagram below showing part of the **small intestine**.

i) ....

ii) ....

iii) ....

iv) ....

b) Explain how the following aid absorption of food:

i) millions of finger-like projections ....
....

ii) very long length ....
....

Q8 Abi set up an experiment as shown to investigate how the **small intestine** works. She tested the liquids at A and B for starch and glucose. Abi then added **amylase** (which digests starch) to the tubing, and tested the liquids again after an hour. The results are shown in the table.

A partially permeable membrane is similar to the wall of the small intestine.

partially permeable membrane

A — starch + amylase

B — water

	Result of starch test	
Liquid	**Before adding amylase**	**An hour after adding amylase**
A	Positive	Negative
B	Negative	Negative

	Result of glucose test	
Liquid	**Before adding amylase**	**An hour after adding amylase**
A	Negative	Positive
B	Negative	Positive

a) Explain why there is no starch at **A** after an hour.
....
....

b) Explain why glucose was detected at **B** after an hour.
....
....

Top Tips: Things tend to spread out — that's all that diffusion is — and in and out of cells, it's no different. Substances will move across the membrane from an area of higher concentration to an area of lower concentration — but only if they're small enough to get through.

Module B3 — Living and Growing

Functions of the Blood

Q1 Tick the correct boxes to show whether these statements are **true** or **false**.

True False

a) The function of red blood cells is to fight germs. ☐ ☐

b) White blood cells help to clot blood. ☐ ☐

c) Glucose can be found in the blood. ☐ ☐

d) The liquid part of blood is called urine. ☐ ☐

e) Platelets help to seal wounds to prevent blood loss. ☐ ☐

Q2 **Plasma** carries just about everything around the body.

a) For each of the substances listed in the table, state where in the body it is travelling **from** and **to**.

Substance	Travelling from	Travelling to
Urea		
Carbon dioxide		
Glucose		

b) List six other things that are carried by plasma.

1. ....
2. ....
3. ....
4. ....
5. ....
6. ....

Q3 Draw a diagram to show how **white blood cells** are able to digest micro-organisms.

Q4 Use the words below to complete the passage about the structure of **red blood cells**.

| large | small | nucleus | flexible | rigid |
| carbon dioxide | oxygen | cytoplasm | haemoglobin | oxyhaemoglobin |

Red blood cells are biconcave in shape, which means they have a .... surface area for absorbing oxygen. They have no ...., but their cytoplasm is full of ...., which can combine with .... to form .... Red blood cells are very ...., which means that they can fit easily through capillaries.

Module B3 — Living and Growing

Circulatory System: Blood Vessels

Q1   Draw lines to match each of the words below with its correct description.

artery

capillary

cholesterol

lumen

vein

fatty substance

hole in the middle of a tube

microscopic blood vessel

vessel that takes blood towards the heart

vessel that takes blood away from the heart

Q2   Circle the correct word in each of the sentences below.

a)   Arteries / Veins contain valves to prevent the blood going backwards.

b)   Capillaries / Veins have walls that are permeable.

c)   Arteries / Capillaries have smooth muscle in their walls.

d)   The blood pressure in the arteries / veins is higher than in the arteries / veins.

Q3   **Cholesterol** is a fatty substance needed in the body.

a)   Why do we need cholesterol in our body? ....

b)   Complete the following sentence.

A diet high in .... **has been linked to high levels of cholesterol in the blood.**

c)   Describe what might happen if you have too much cholesterol in your body.

....

....

Q4   Gareth did an experiment to compare the elasticity of **arteries** and **veins**. He dissected out an artery and a vein from a piece of fresh meat. He then took a 5 cm length of each vessel, hung different masses on it, and measured how much it stretched. His results are shown in the table.

a)   Suggest one way in which Gareth could tell which was the artery and which was the vein when he was dissecting the meat.

....

....

mass added (g)	length of blood vessel (mm)	
	artery	vein
0	50	50
5	51	53
10	53	56
15	55	59
20	56	-

b)   If Gareth plots his results on a graph, which variable should he put on the vertical axis, and why?

....

c)   Which vessel stretched more easily? Explain why this was.

....

d)   Why did he take both vessels from the same piece of meat?

....

Circulatory System: The Heart

Q1 The diagram below shows the human **heart**, as seen from the front.
The left atrium has been labelled. Complete the remaining labels a) to j).

a) ....

b) ....

c) ....

d) ....

e) ....

f) ....

g) ....

left atrium

h) ....

i) ....

j) ....

Q2 A red blood cell is in the **aorta**. It circulates around the body and passes through each of the following structures. Number these structures from 1 to 8 in the order in which they are reached.

☐ left atrium   ☐ left ventricle   ☐ lungs   ☐ pulmonary artery

☐ pulmonary vein   ☐ right atrium   ☐ right ventricle   ☐ vena cava

Q3 Tick the boxes to say whether each statement below is **true** or **false**.

True False

a) Arteries always carry oxygenated blood. ☐ ☐

b) Blood vessels taking blood to and from the lungs are called pulmonary vessels. ☐ ☐

c) The atria of the heart have thicker walls than the ventricles. ☐ ☐

d) The right side of the heart pumps deoxygenated blood. ☐ ☐

e) Valves prevent blood flowing backwards. ☐ ☐

Q4 Mammals have a **double** circulatory system in which blood is pumped by the **heart**.

a) Explain the meaning of the term **double circulation**.

....

b) Name a group of vertebrates that does **not** have a double circulation. ....

c) What is the advantage of a double circulatory system?

....

d) Explain why the wall of the left ventricle is thicker than the wall of the right ventricle.

....

....

Replacement Hearts

Q1 Complete the passage using some of the words provided below.

> artificial   chambers   vena cava
> irregular   pacemaker   valves   regular

> The rate at which the heart beats is determined by the ....
>
> Sometimes, this stops working properly, and the heartbeat becomes
>
> .... In this case, an .... unit is fitted.
>
> Defective heart .... can also be replaced.

Q2 Match the words to their correct descriptions.

rejection	someone who provides an organ for transplantation
transplant	the structure that determines how fast the heart beats
donor	a structure in the heart that stops blood going backwards
valve	when the immune system attacks a transplanted organ
pacemaker	when an organ in a person is replaced with a new organ

Q3 Read the descriptions of the following patients before choosing a suitable treatment from the list.

replacement valve from a pig   battery-operated pacemaker

artificial replacement valve   complete heart transplant

a) Annie has an irregular heartbeat, but is otherwise healthy.

....

b) Alistair has a heart valve that is allowing blood to flow backwards through it.
He also once had a dangerous blood clot in the leg.

....

c) Clive has a damaged heart valve. He is known to react badly to the drugs
that are normally used to suppress the immune system.

....

d) Valerie is a 40 year old woman, who has a badly diseased heart.
She is in danger of dying very soon if she is not treated.

....

Replacement Hearts

Q4 In the UK, some patients who need heart transplants don't get them because there aren't enough suitable **donor hearts** available.

    a) Describe **two** reasons why there aren't enough suitable hearts available for donation.

....

....

    b) Suggest a way in which the supply of donor hearts could be increased.

....

Q5 The table below shows the number of **heart transplants** carried out in Cloudyford.

Year	1996	1997	1998	1999	2000	2001	2002	2003	2004	2005
No. heart transplants	36	35	35	31	30	27	24	21	26	20

    a) Plot these figures as a bar chart on the grid opposite.

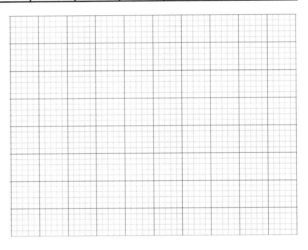

    b) Describe how the number of heart transplants has changed over time.

....

....

    c) Instead of a complete heart transplant, surgeons sometimes decide to replace only a part of the heart, such as a valve. Give **two** reasons why this is often better for the patient.

....

....

    d) Suggest why the future number of transplants carried out in Cloudyford may:

      i) increase. ....

      ii) decrease. ....

Multiplying Cells

Q1   Choose from the following words to complete the passage below.

haploid   mitosis   nucleus   meiosis   two   one   cytoplasm   diploid

DNA is found inside the .... of each cell. When a human grows, the individual

cells grow and then divide by a process called .... All human body cells are

..........................., which means they contain .... copies of each chromosome.

Reproductive cells are formed by a process called .... These cells are

..........................., which means they contain .... copy of each chromosome.

Q2   The following diagram shows the different stages of **mitosis**.
Write a short description to explain each stage.

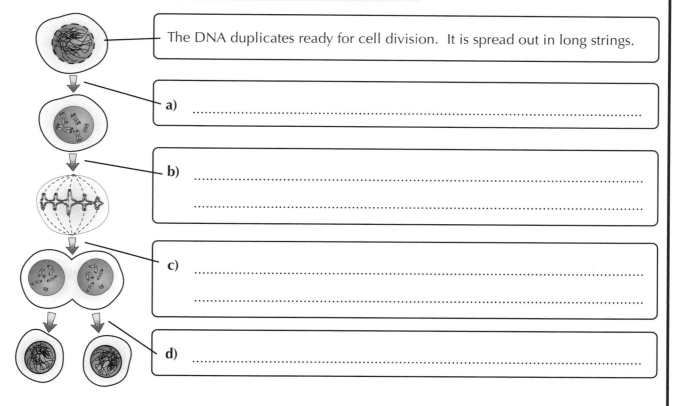

The DNA duplicates ready for cell division. It is spread out in long strings.

a) ....

b) ....
....

c) ....
....

d) ....

Q3   Explain two advantages of being **multi-cellular** compared to being **single-celled**.

1. ....

....

2. ....

....

Multiplying Cells

Q4 Bacteria can divide every **30 minutes**. A **single** bacterial cell is left to multiply.

How many bacteria will there be after:

a) 30 minutes? ....

b) 1 hours? ....

c) 3 hours? ....

Billy...?

Q5 Barry cut off the tip of a **plant root** and squashed it on a microscope slide. He added a chemical stain that attaches to DNA and then viewed the slide under a **microscope**. Below is a diagram representing what he saw.

a) Suggest why Barry:

i) squashed the root tip. ....

ii) added the stain. ....

b) Describe what is happening in the cell pointed to by an arrow?

....

Q6 Eddie makes some cubes to represent different sized cells.

To calculate the surface area to volume ratio, divide the surface area by the volume.

a) Calculate the surface area, volume and surface area to volume ratio for each cube.

Size (cm)	Surface area (cm^2)	Volume (cm^3)	Surface area to volume ratio
2 × 2 × 2			
4 × 4 × 4			
6 × 6 × 6			
8 × 8 × 8			

b) Describe the trend in surface area to volume ratio.

....

c) Use these results to explain why single-celled organisms can't grow very large.

....

....

Sexual Reproduction

Q1   Match the following adaptations of **sperm cells** to how they help the sperm fertilise the egg.

acrosome containing enzymes

produced in large numbers

small with long tails

lots of mitochondria

to provide the energy needed to move

to digest the membrane of the egg cell

so they can swim to the egg

to increase the chance of fertilisation

Q2   Draw lines to match the diagrams of each stage of **meiosis** to the right descriptions below.

a)

b)

c)

d)

e)

The pairs are pulled apart, mixing up the mother and father's chromosomes into the new cells. This creates genetic variation.

Before the cell starts to divide it duplicates its DNA to produce an exact copy.

There are now 4 gametes, each containing half the original number of chromosomes.

For the first meiotic division the chromosomes line up in their pairs across the centre of the cell.

The chromosomes line up across the centre of the nucleus ready for the second division, and the left and right arms are pulled apart.

Q3   During sexual reproduction, two **gametes** combine to form a new individual.

a)   What are gametes? ....

b)   Explain why it is important that gametes have half the usual number of chromosomes.

....

....

c)   Explain how we get genetic variation in meiotic cell division.

....

....

Stem Cells and Differentiation

Q1   The following terms are related to **stem cells**. Explain what each term means.

a)   specialised cells ....

b)   differentiation ....

c)   undifferentiated cells ....

Q2   Give two differences in **growth** between plants and animals.

1. ....

2. ....

Q3   In the future, **embryonic stem cells** might be used to replace faulty cells in sick people.

a)   How are **embryonic** stem cells different from **adult** stem cells?

....

....

b)   Describe one way that stem cells are already used in medicine.

....

....

c)   Match the problems below to the potential cures which could be developed using stem cells.

diabetes	heart muscle cells
paralysis	insulin-producing cells
heart disease	brain cells
Alzheimer's	nerve cells

Q4   People have **different opinions** when it comes to **stem cell research**.

a)   Give one argument **in favour** of stem cell research.

....

....

b)   Give one argument **against** stem cell research.

....

....

Growth in Humans

Q1 Some animals give birth to **live** young.

a) Define the term '**gestation**'.

....

....

b) What class of animals have a gestation period? ....

c) Give two factors that determine the length of gestation.

1. ....

2. ....

Q2 Complete the following table showing the stages in the normal **human life span**.

	Stage	Description
Birth →		
Death →		

Q3 The graph below shows how the **average growth rate** of girls and boys varies between the ages of 2 and 24.

a) At what age range is the greatest **adolescent** growth rate for:

i) boys? ....

ii) girls? ....

Adolescence is usually between 10 and 19 years.

b) **i)** At what age does growth stop for girls on average? ....

ii) How is this indicated on the graph?

....

Key:
Girls
Boys

Growth Rate (cm per year)

Age (years)

Q4 During childhood, Angela's height increased from 110 cm at 5 years old to 140 cm at 9 years old.

Calculate her average growth rate during this period in cm per year. Show your working.

....

....

Growth in Humans

Q5 The diagram below shows how the proportions of the human body change with age.

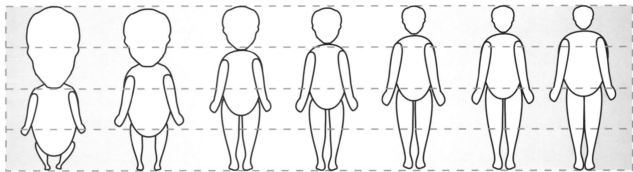

| 7 months before birth | 4 months before birth | at birth | 2 years old | 6 years old | 12 years old | 25 years old |

Approximately what proportion of the total body height is taken up by the head at:

a) 7 months before birth? ....

b) at birth? ....

c) at 25 years? ....

Q6 Zapphites from the planet Zaphron have a similar growth pattern to humans. The graph shows the **head circumference** of baby Zapphites between birth and 40 weeks. The shaded area shows where 90% of babies fall.

Baby's name	Age (weeks)	Head circumference (cm)
Charles	19	46.5
Edward	15	51
Engletree	34	54
George	27	49
Henry	23	49
Oliver	29	57
Richard	39	50
Xionbert	23	51.5

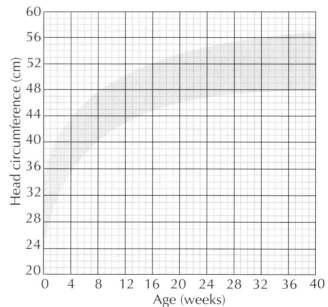

a) Plot the head circumferences of the above babies on the graph.

b) Why might Zapphite doctors monitor a baby's head circumference? ....

....

c) Which baby's head size may cause concern? ....

Module B3 — Living and Growing

Growth in Plants

Q1 Decide whether the following statements are **true** or **false**.

True False

a) Plant shoots grow away from light. ☐ ☐

b) Plant roots grow towards light. ☐ ☐

c) Plant roots grow in the same direction that gravity acts. ☐ ☐

d) If the tip of a shoot is removed, the shoot may stop growing upwards. ☐ ☐

Q2 Choose the correct word or phrase from each pair to complete the following paragraph.

When a shoot tip is exposed to light from one side, auxin accumulates on the side that's in the **light / shade**. This makes the cells grow **faster / slower** on the shaded side, so the shoot bends **away from / towards** the light. When a root is exposed to light from one side, auxin accumulates on the side that's in the **light / shade**. This makes the cells grow **faster / slower** on the shaded side, so the root bends **downwards / upwards**.

Q3 Two shoot tips were removed from young plants. Agar blocks soaked in auxin were placed on the cut ends of the shoots as shown in the diagram, and placed in the dark.

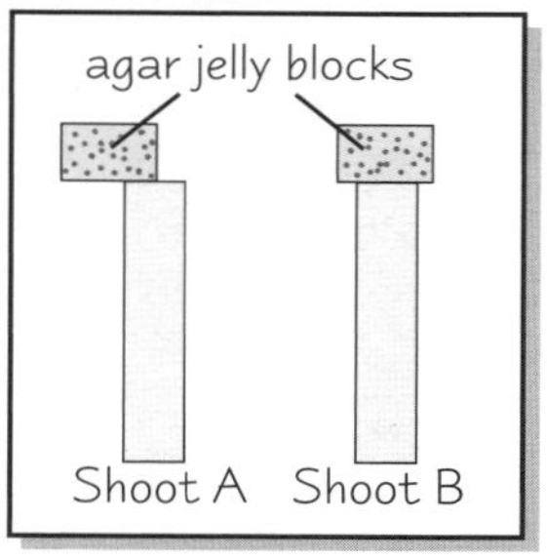

a) Describe the expected responses of shoots A and B to this treatment.

i) Shoot A ....

ii) Shoot B ....

agar jelly blocks

Shoot A   Shoot B

b) Explain your answers.

i) Shoot A ....

....

i) Shoot B ....

....

Q4 **Auxin** affect plant shoots and roots differently.

a) Describe the **difference** between how auxin affects cells in the shoots and in the roots of plants.

....

....

b) Some side roots of plants grow at an angle to the main root, instead of straight down under the influence of gravity. Suggest why this might be an **advantage** for the plant.

....

Growth in Plants

Q5 Cedrick placed some **seedlings** on the surface of **damp soil** and left them for **five days**. The appearance of a seedling is shown in the diagram.

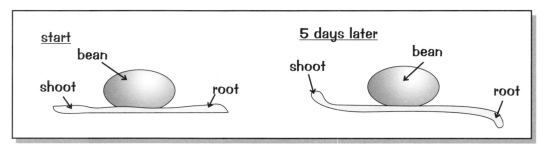

a) What **hormones** are responsible for these changes? ....

b) Where are these hormones produced? ....

c) Explain the results observed for the shoot and the root in terms of their response to **gravity**.

    i) the shoot ....

    ....

    ii) the root ....

    ....

Q6 Vicky used three seedlings to investigate plant growth. Each seedling was prepared differently (see table). All three were placed in the same conditions, exposed to light from **one** direction and left for five hours. She recorded her results in the table below.

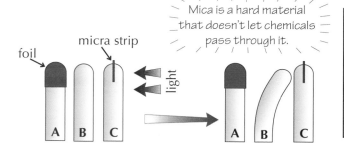

Mica is a hard material that doesn't let chemicals pass through it.

Seedling	Preparation	Observation after 5 hours
A	foil covering tip	no change
B	left alone	tip bent towards the light
C	mica strip through centre of tip	no change

a) Suggest why seedling A and seedling C failed to respond to the light.

Seedling A ....

....

Seedling C ....

....

b) Suggest how the experiment could be improved.

....

Commercial Use of Plant Hormones

Q1 Describe four ways in which **plant hormones** can be used **commercially**.

1. ....

2. ....

3. ....

4. ....

Q2 Ronald owns a fruit farm which grows satsumas. The fruit is picked before it is ripe and transported to market.

fruit picked ➡ fruit packaged ➡ fruit transported to market ➡ fruit displayed

a) Suggest why the satsumas are picked before they are ripe.

....

....

b) i) How could the unripened satsumas be ripened in time to reach the market?

....

ii) At what stage in the diagram above should the satsumas be ripened?

....

Q3 Charlie sprayed a batch of **dormant** barley seeds with a dilute solution of a plant hormone. This caused all the seeds to germinate.

a) Define the term **dormancy**.

....

b) Name the plant hormone in the solution. ....

c) Suggest two reasons why it is useful to be able to control when seeds germinate.

....

....

Module B3 — Living and Growing

Commercial Use of Plant Hormones

Q4 Sanjay owns two neighbouring fields — **Field A** and **Field B**. They are an identical size, have the same soil and he uses the same fertiliser regime for both. The only difference is that he applies a weedkiller containing plant growth hormones to Field B but not Field A.

This table shows the yields for both fields.

Year	1997	1998	1999	2000	2001
Barley yield from field A, kg/ha	35	28	33	37	34
Barley yield from field B, kg/ha	48	39	44	49	43

a) What effect did the weedkiller have on crop yield?

....

b) Explain how this type of weedkiller works.

....

....

Q5 Barry is investigating the effect of **auxin concentration** on the growth of the roots in some **identical plant cuttings**. His measurements are shown in the table.

a) What are plant cuttings? ....

b) Complete the table by calculating the increase in root length at each concentration.

Concentration of auxin (parts per million)	0	0.001	0.01	0.1	1
Length of root at start of investigation (mm)	20	20	20	20	20
Length of root 1 week after investigation started (mm)	26	32	28	23	21
Increase of root length (mm)					

c) Plot a bar chart of the concentration of auxin against the increase in root length on the graph paper.

d) What do the results suggest is the best concentration of auxin to use to encourage growth?

....

e) What do you notice about the effect of high auxin concentration on the rate of growth?

....

....

f) Give one way in which Barry has helped to make this a fair test.

....

<u>Mutation</u>

Q1 Tick the correct boxes to show whether the following statements are **true** or **false**.

True False

a) Mutations are always harmful.

b) Mutations can occur spontaneously.

c) Mutations can prevent the production of a protein.

d) Mutations occurring in body cells are passed on to offspring.

e) Cigarette smoke contains mutagens.

Q2 Complete the following paragraph using the words below.

a different protein	gene	base sequence	no protein	replication

Mutagens change the .... of DNA. If this change becomes permanent

(through DNA ....), it becomes a mutation. If this mutation occurs within a

....................., you could end up with .... or

.... produced.

Q3 Suggest explanations for the following facts.

a) In 1986, a nuclear reactor at Chernobyl in the Ukraine exploded. Afterwards, the rate of thyroid cancer amongst children in the surrounding region increased by approximately 1000%.

....

....

b) If fruit flies with normal wings are given high doses of X-rays, they are apparently unharmed. However, when they breed, they produce a completely new variety of fruit fly with short wings.

....

....

c) Smokers are more likely to suffer from lung cancer than non-smokers.

....

....

Q4 Explain why a **beneficial** mutation is likely to be passed on to the next generation.

....

....

....

Selective Breeding

Q1 Garfield wants to breed one type of plant for its **fruit**, and another as an **ornamental house plant**.

Suggest **two** characteristics that he should select for in each kind of plant.

Fruit plant: ....

Ornamental house plant: ....

Q2 Describe two long term **disadvantages** of selective breeding.

1. ....

....

2. ....

....

Q3 Many breeds of **domesticated dog** have been bred for their **friendly temperament**.

a) Describe how selective breeding from an **aggressive** wolf-like stock of dogs could produce a breed with a more **friendly** temperament.

....

....

b) Explain why some domesticated dog breeds are likely to suffer from genetic disorders.

....

....

Q4 The graph shows the **milk yield** for a population of cows over three generations.

a) Do you think that selective breeding is likely to have been used with these cows? Explain your answer.

....

....

b) What is the increase in the average milk yield per cow from generation 1 to generation 2?

....

Key: Generation 1 ——— Generation 2 ——— Generation 3 ———

Number of cows / Milk yield / litres produced per year per cow

---

Top Tips: So, if you wanted to take over the world using goldfish, you would probably want to breed together the more aggressive goldfish with long memories, rather than the dappy ones that just idly swim around in a circle all day long. (You can tell which ones are aggressive — they bite.)

Genetic Engineering

Q1   **Human insulin** can be produced quickly using **genetic engineering**.

 a)   Put these stages in the production of human insulin in order by numbering them 1–4.

☐ The human insulin gene is inserted into the host DNA of a bacterium.

☐ The human insulin gene is cut from human DNA.

☐ Insulin is extracted from the medium.

☐ The bacteria are cultivated in a fermenter.

 b)   Suggest an **advantage** of using bacteria to produce insulin.

....

Q2   Plants can be genetically engineered.

 a)   Describe how genetic engineering could improve crop yield.

....

 b)   Describe how genetic engineering can help people get the vitamins they need.

....

....

Q3   Some people are **worried** about genetic engineering.

 a)   Explain why this is.

....

....

 b)   Do you think that scientists should be carrying out genetic engineering? Explain your answer.

....

....

....

Q4   Look carefully at this headline about a new type of **GM salmon**.

Monster food? Scientists insert a growth hormone gene and create fish that grow much faster than ever before!

Some scientists have warned that the GM salmon should be tightly controlled so they don't escape into the sea. What might happen if the GM salmon were allowed to escape?

....

....

Cloning: Embryo Transplants

Q1   Define the following terms.

a)   Clone ....

b)   Surrogate mother ....

c)   Embryo ....

d)   Artificial insemination ....

Q2   Joe has a herd of cows and he wants them all to have calves,
but he **only** wants to breed from his champion bull and prize cow.

a)   Name a method Joe could use to achieve this. ....

b)   Describe the steps involved in this method in detail.

....

....

....

....

c)   Which of the animals involved in this process will be genetically identical?

....

d)   Give one disadvantage of this method.

....

....

Q3   Read the passage before deciding whether the statements that follow are **true** or **false**.

> Sperm was collected from Gerald the stallion and used to artificially inseminate
> Daisy the mare. An embryo was then removed from Daisy and divided into
> separate cells, each of which was allowed to grow into a new embryo. These new
> embryos were then implanted into other horses, including Rosie, Ruby and Jilly.

	True	False
a) Each embryo is genetically identical to Daisy.	☐	☐
b) Gerald is genetically identical to the embryos.	☐	☐
c) All the embryos are genetically identical.	☐	☐
d) The embryo carried by Jilly is her natural daughter.	☐	☐
e) All the embryos carry some of Daisy's genes.	☐	☐

Module B3 — Living and Growing

Adult Cloning

Q1   **Dolly** the sheep was cloned from an adult cell.

a)   Write the correct letter (A, B, C or D) next to each label below to show where it belongs on the diagram.

removing and discarding a nucleus ....

implantation in a surrogate mother ....

useful nucleus extracted ....

formation of a diploid cell ....

b)   What type of cell division does the fertilised egg divide by? ....

c)   Give a risk associated with this type of cloning.

....

Q2   Some animals can be genetically engineered to produce **human blood clotting agents**.

a)   Why would it be useful to be able to clone these animals?

....

....

b)   Suggest why some people might be reluctant to use medicines produced by cloned animals.

....

Q3   Adult cloning may help to make **xenotransplantation** safe.

a)   What is xenotransplantation?

....

b)   Explain the possible role of cloning in xenotransplantation.

....

....

Q4   Summarise the **ethical** issues involved in cloning humans.

....

....

....

Cloning Plants: Asexual Reproduction

Q1 Rachel has a flowering plant with especially attractive characteristics.
She decides to clone it by taking **cuttings**.

  a) What is this method of **reproduction** called? ....

  b) Explain why:

    i) cuttings from a plant are **clones** of each other.

    ....

    ii) Rachel chose to reproduce her plant in this way, rather than letting it produce seeds.

    ....

    ....

    iii) cloning is **easier** to do in plants than in animals.

    ....

  c) Give one **disadvantage** of using this method of reproduction.

  ....

  ....

  d) Give **two** examples of plants that can produce clones **naturally**.

  1. .... 2. ....

Q2 Plants can be cloned by a method called **tissue culture**. This involves taking clusters of cells from a parent plant and letting each cluster grow into a new plant.

  a) What would be the best part of the plant from which to take the cell clusters? Explain your answer.

  ....

  b) Explain why tissue culture is likely to be able to produce more clones from a plant than taking cuttings is.

  ....

Q3 Some plants are being grown using tissue culture.

  a) Name two substances that the jelly contains to help the young plants grow successfully.

jelly

  1. .... 2. ....

  b) Why is the tissue grown under aseptic conditions?

  ....

Mixed Questions — Module B3

Q1   Both **plants** and **animals** are made up of cells.

a)   Complete this diagram of a plant cell by filling in the labels.

....

....

....

b)   Name the part of the cell:

    i)   where energy is released from glucose, ...

    ii)   which contains chlorophyll for photosynthesis, ...

    iii) which contains genetic material, ...

    iv)   which provides support.   ....

c)   Name three parts that are found in plant cells but not in animal cells.

    1. ....   2. ....   3. ....

d)   Describe how plant growth differs from animal growth regarding:

    i)   cell enlargement   ....

        ....

    ii)   cell division   ....

        ....

    iii) cell differentiation   ....

        ....

Q2   Scientists tried to **genetically modify** some bacteria. They inserted a piece of DNA containing both the human gene for **growth hormone** and a gene for **penicillin resistance** into a bacterium. Afterwards, the bacteria were grown on agar plates containing penicillin.

a)   Why were the bacteria grown on plates containing penicillin?

Hint: It's hard to tell by looking if the growth hormone gene has been inserted correctly.

....

....

b)   Give **two advantages** of producing growth hormone with bacteria, rather than by other methods.

....

....

Mixed Questions — Module B3

Q3   **Gas exchange** happens in the lungs.

a)   Name the **air sacs** responsible for gas exchange. ....

    When affected by a disease called **emphysema**, the structure of these air sacs changes as shown.

    normal air sac   air sac with emphysema

b)   What effect does emphysema have on the surface area of the air sacs?

....

c)   Explain why people with emphysema are given oxygen to breathe.

....

....

....

Q4   The diagram shows two **processes** that occur in the human body.

a)   Name the type of **cell division** that occurs in:

    i)   Process X: ....

    ii)   Process Y: ....

b)   Which process produces:

    i)   Genetically **identical** cells? ....

    ii)   Genetically **different** cells? ....

X Body cell → Body cells

Y Body cell → Gametes

c)   Give an example of what process **X** might be used for.

....

Q5   The sequence of bases in part of one strand of a **DNA** molecule is as follows:

A–A–T–C–C–A–A–T–C

a)   Write down the **complementary sequence** of bases on the other strand of DNA.

....

b)   Describe the relationship between DNA and proteins.

....

....

Module B3 — Living and Growing

Mixed Questions — Module B3

Q6 a) What unique characteristic do **stem cells** have which ordinary body cells don't have?

....

b) Scientists have experimented with growing stem cells in different conditions. What is the name of the process by which stem cells **divide** for growth?

....

c) Suggest why scientists are especially interested in **embryonic** stem cells.

....

....

d) Although there is potential for medical breakthroughs, some people disagree with stem cell research on ethical grounds. Describe one **ethical issue** surrounding stem cell research.

....

....

Q7 The diagram shows part of the circulatory system.

a) Name the blood vessels labelled W, X, Y and Z.

W ....

X ....

Y ....

Z ....

b) State one difference in composition between the blood entering the heart from the vena cava and the blood leaving the heart through the aorta.

....

c) Explain how the structure of an artery is adapted for its function.

....

....

d) i) Which type of blood vessel contains valves? ....

ii) What is the function of these valves?

....

Mixed Questions — Module B3

Q8 "Dolly the sheep" was produced in 1997 in Edinburgh, and was the world's first clone of an adult mammal. The diagram illustrates the process by which clones like Dolly can be produced.

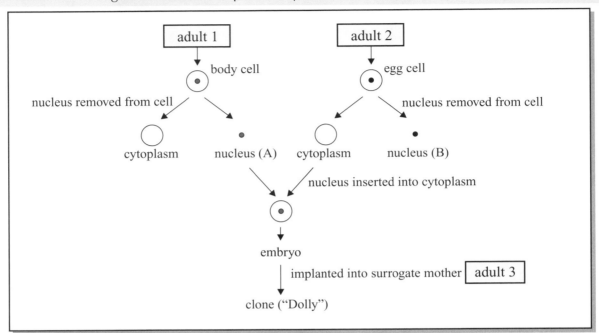

a) In the diagram above, which adult (1, 2 or 3) will the clone be identical to, and why?

....

....

b) An unfertilised sheep's egg contains 27 chromosomes. How many chromosomes will there be in:

i) the nucleus labelled A: ....

ii) the nucleus labelled B: ....

iii) the cloned sheep's body cells: ....

c) Explain why this cloning process is potentially more useful to animal breeders than selective breeding or embryo transplants.

....

....

Q9 The **Jungle Fowl** is the wild ancestor of all farm-bred chickens.
Farm-bred chickens have been produced by **selective breeding**.

a) Suggest two ways in which farm-bred chickens are likely to differ from wild Jungle Fowl.

1. .... 2. ....

b) Suggest how selective breeding in chickens might harm the welfare of the birds.

....

....

Chemical Equations

Q1   Are the following statements **true** or **false**? Tick the correct boxes.

                                                                                 True False

   a)   Displayed formulas show all the atoms and covalent bonds in a molecule. □ □

   b)   During a chemical reaction no atoms are lost or made. □ □

   c)   There are three carbon atoms in a molecule of C_4H_{10}. □ □

   d)   There is one oxygen atom in a molecule of C_3H_7OH. □ □

Q2   **Potassium** reacts with **bromine** to form **potassium bromide**.

   a)   What are the **reactant(s)** and the **product(s)** in this reaction?

       Reactant(s): ....   Product(s): ....

   b)   Write the **word equation** for this reaction.

       ....

Q3   A book describes a reaction as follows: "**Methane** (CH_4) burns in **oxygen** (O_2) to form **carbon dioxide** (CO_2) and **water** (H_2O)."

   a)   What are the **reactants** and the **products** in this reaction?

       Reactants: ....   Products: ....

   b)   Write the **word equation** for this reaction.

       ....

Q4   Complete the table on the right showing the **displayed formulas** and **molecular formulas** of three carbon compounds.

DISPLAYED FORMULA	MOLECULAR FORMULA
H | H—C—H | H	a)
H H | | H—C—C—H | | H H	b)
H H H | | | H—C—C—C—H | | | H H H	c)

Q5   **Methanol** has the molecular formula CH_3OH.

       Draw the **displayed formula** for methanol in the box opposite.

Balancing Equations

Q1 Which of the following equations are **balanced** correctly?

Correctly balanced   Incorrectly balanced

a) $CuO + HCl \rightarrow CuCl_2 + H_2O$ ☐   ☐

b) $N_2 + H_2 \rightarrow NH_3$ ☐   ☐

c) $CuO + H_2 \rightarrow Cu + H_2O$ ☐   ☐

d) $CaCO_3 \rightarrow CaO + CO_2$ ☐   ☐

e) $Al + Fe_2O_3 \rightarrow Al_2O_3 + Fe$ ☐   ☐

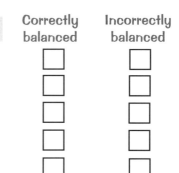

Q2 Here is the equation for the production of carbon **mon**oxide from a poorly ventilated charcoal flame. It is **not** balanced correctly.

$$C + O_2 \rightarrow CO$$

Circle the **correctly balanced** version of this equation.

$$C + O_2 \rightarrow CO_2$$

$$C + O_2 \rightarrow 2CO$$

$$2C + O_2 \rightarrow 2CO$$

Q3 Follow the steps to find the formula of **iron(II) carbonate**.

a) What is the charge on an iron(II) ion? ....

b) What is the charge on a carbonate ion? ....

c) What is the formula of iron(II) carbonate? ....

Q4 Use the table to work out the **formulas** of the following compounds.

Positive Ions			Negative Ions	
Lithium Li$^+$	Barium Ba^{2+}	Zinc Zn^{2+}	Chloride Cl$^-$
Sodium Na$^+$	Magnesium Mg^{2+}	Manganese(II) Mn^{2+}	Hydroxide OH$^-$
Potassium K$^+$	Iron(II) Fe^{2+}	Aluminium Al^{3+}	Oxide O^{2-}
	Copper(II) Cu^{2+}	Iron(III) Fe^{3+}	Carbonate CO$_3^{2-}$

a) magnesium oxide ....

b) potassium chloride ....

c) copper(II) carbonate ....

d) sodium hydroxide ....

e) iron(III) hydroxide ....

Balancing Equations

Q5 Write out the balanced **symbol** equations for the picture equations below (some of which are unbalanced).

a) Na + Cl Cl → Na Cl

....

You can draw more pictures to help you balance the unbalanced ones.

b) Li + O O → Li O Li

....

c) Mg O O C O + H Cl → Cl Mg Cl + H O H + O C O

....

d) Li + H O H → Li O H + H H

....

Q6 Add **one** number to each of these equations so that they are **correctly balanced**.

a) .... CuO + ... HBr → .... $CuBr_2$ + ... H_2O

b) .... H_2 + ... Br_2 → .... HBr

c) .... Mg + ... O_2 → $2MgO$

d) $2NaOH$ + ... H_2SO_4 → .... Na_2SO_4 + ... H_2O

I've left spaces in front of all the molecules so I don't give the game away. If a molecule doesn't need a number in front, just leave it blank.

Q7 **Balance** these equations.

a) .... $NaOH$ + ... $AlBr_3$ → .... $NaBr$ + ... $Al(OH)_3$

b) .... $FeCl_2$ + ... Cl_2 → .... $FeCl_3$

c) .... N_2 + ... H_2 → .... NH_3

d) .... Fe + ... O_2 → .... Fe_2O_3

e) .... NH_3 + ... O_2 → .... NO + ... H_2O

$Fe_2O_3 + 3CO → 2Fe + 3CO_2$

Top Tip: Balancing equations is a simple matter of **trial and error** — keep changing one thing at a time until eventually you get the same number of each atom on both sides.

__Atoms__

Q1 **Complete** the following sentences.

a) Neutral atoms have a charge of ....

b) A charged atom is called an ....

c) A neutral atom has the same number of .... and ....

d) If an electron is added to a neutral atom, the atom becomes .... charged.

Q2 **Complete** this table.

Particle	Mass	Charge
Proton	1	
	1	0
Electron		−1

Q3 **What am I?**

Choose from: **nucleus   proton   electron   neutron**

a) I am in the centre of the atom. I contain protons and neutrons. ....

b) I move around the nucleus in a shell. ....

c) I am the lightest. ....

d) I am positively charged. ....

e) I am relatively heavy and have no charge. ....

f) In a neutral atom there are as many of me as there are electrons. ....

Q4 Elements have a **mass number** and an **atomic number**.

a) What does the **mass number** of an element tell you?

....

b) What does the **atomic number** of an element tell you?

....

c) Fill in this table using a periodic table.

Element	Symbol	Mass Number	Number of Protons	Number of Electrons	Number of Neutrons
Sodium	Na		11		
		16	8	8	8
Neon			10	10	10
	Ca			20	20

Isotopes, Elements and Compounds

Q1 a) Correctly label the following diagrams with either 'element' or 'compound'.

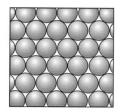 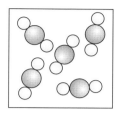 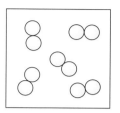 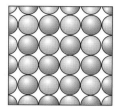

A = ...   B = ...   C = ...   D= ....

b) Suggest which diagram (A, B, C or D) could represent:

    i) oxygen ....   **ii)** sodium ....   **iii)** sodium chloride ....   **iv)** carbon dioxide ....

Q2   Circle the **correct words** in these sentences.

a) Compounds / Atoms are formed when two or more elements react together.

b) The properties of compounds are **exactly the same as** / **completely different to** those of the original elements.

c) It is **easy** / **difficult** to separate the elements in a compound.

d) Carbon dioxide is **a compound** / **an element**, whereas iron is **a compound** / **an element**.

e) The number of **neutrons** / **electrons** determines the chemistry of an element.

Q3   Choose the correct words to **complete** this paragraph.

element	isotopes	protons	neutrons

.... are different atomic forms of the same .... which have the same number of .... but a different number of ....

Q4   Which of the following atoms are **isotopes** of each other? Explain your answer.

W $\begin{array}{l}12\\6\end{array}\text{C}$ **X** $\begin{array}{l}4\\2\end{array}\text{He}$ **Y** $\begin{array}{l}14\\6\end{array}\text{C}$ **Z** $\begin{array}{l}14\\7\end{array}\text{N}$

Answer: .... and ....

Explanation: ....

Q5   Describe the following types of **chemical bonding**:

a) Ionic ....

b) Covalent ....

The Periodic Table

Q1   Select from these **elements** to answer the following questions.

iodine   nickel   silicon   sodium   radon   krypton   calcium

a)   Which two elements are in the same group? .... and ....

b)   Name two elements which are in Period 3. .... and ....

c)   Name an alkali metal. ....

d)   Name a transition metal. ....

e)   Name an element with seven electrons in its outer shell. ....

f)   Name a non-metal which is not in Group 8. ....

Q2   Tick the correct boxes to show whether these statements are **true** or **false**.

		True	False
a)	Elements in the same **group** have the same number of electrons in their outer shell.	☐	☐
b)	The periodic table shows the elements in order of ascending **atomic mass**.	☐	☐
c)	Each **column** in the periodic table contains elements with similar properties.	☐	☐
d)	The periodic table is made up of all the known compounds.	☐	☐
e)	There are more than 100 known elements.	☐	☐
f)	Each new period in the periodic table represents another full shell of electrons.	☐	☐

Q3   Elements in the same group undergo **similar reactions**.

a)   Tick the pairs of elements that would undergo similar reactions.

A potassium and rubidium   ☐   **C** calcium and oxygen   ☐

B helium and fluorine   ☐   **D** nitrogen and arsenic   ☐

b)   Explain why fluorine and chlorine undergo similar reactions.

....

....

Q4   Complete the following table.

	Alternative Name	Number of Electrons in Outer Shell
Group 1		
Group 7		
Group 8		*

* excluding helium

Electron Shells

Q1 a) Tick the boxes to show whether the statements are **true** or **false**.

True False

i) Electrons occupy shells. ☐ ☐

ii) The highest energy levels are always filled first. ☐ ☐

iii) Atoms are most stable when they have partially filled shells. ☐ ☐

iv) Noble gases have a full outer shell of electrons. ☐ ☐

v) Reactive elements have full outer shells. ☐ ☐

b) Write out corrected versions of the **false** statements.

....

....

....

Q2 Identify **two** things that are wrong with this diagram.

1. ....

....

2. ....

....

Q3 Write out the **electronic configuration** for each of the following elements.

a) Beryllium ....

d) Calcium ....

b) Oxygen ....

e) Aluminium ....

c) Silicon ....

f) Argon ....

Q4 Do the following groups contain **reactive** or **unreactive** elements? Explain your answers in terms of **electron shells**.

a) Noble gases (Group 8) ....

....

b) Alkali metals (Group 1) ....

....

Electron Shells

Q5   **Chlorine** has an atomic number of 17.

a)   What is chlorine's electron configuration? ....

b)   Draw the electrons on the shells in the diagram.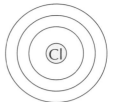

c)   Why does chlorine react readily?

....

Q6   Draw the **full electronic arrangements** for these elements. (The first three have been done for you.)

Hydrogen

Helium

Lithium

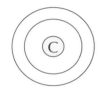

a) Carbon

b) Nitrogen

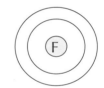

c)   Fluorine

d) Sodium

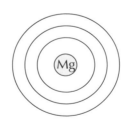

e) Magnesium

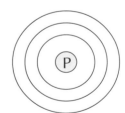

f)   Phosphorus

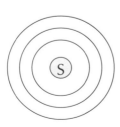

g) Sulfur

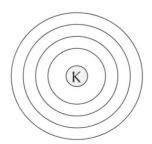

h)   Potassium

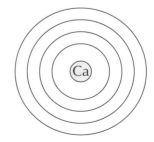

i)   Calcium

Top Tips: Once you've learnt the 'electron shell rules' these are pretty easy — the first shell can only take 2 electrons, and the second and third shells a maximum of 8 each. Don't forget it.

Ionic Bonding

Q1   Fill in the gaps in the sentences below by choosing the correct words from the box.

protons	charged particles	repelled by
electrons	ions	attracted to	neutral particles

a)   In ionic bonding atoms lose or gain .... to form ....

b)   Ions are ....

c)   Ions with opposite charges are strongly .... each other.

Q2   Tick the correct boxes to show whether the following statements are **true** or **false**.

		True	False
a)	Metals have low numbers of electrons in their outer shells.	☐	☐
b)	Metals form negatively charged ions.	☐	☐
c)	Elements in Group 7 gain electrons when they react.	☐	☐
d)	Atoms form ions because they are more stable when they have full outer shells.	☐	☐
e)	Elements in Group 8 are very reactive.	☐	☐

Q3   Use this **diagram** to answer the following questions.

a)   Which **group** of the periodic table does **sodium** belong to? ....

b)   How many **electrons** does **chlorine** need to gain to get a full outer shell of electrons? ....

c)   What is the **charge** on a **sodium ion**? ....

d)   What is the chemical formula of **sodium chloride**? ....

Q4   Here are some elements and the ions they form:

Make sure the charges on the ions balance.

beryllium, Be^{2+} potassium, K^+ iodine, I^- sulfur, S^{2-}

Write down the formulas of four compounds which can be made using these elements.

1. ....   2. ....

3. ....   4. ....

Ions and Ionic Compounds

Q1 Magnesium and oxygen react to form **magnesium oxide**, an **ionic** compound.

a) Draw a 'dot and cross' diagram showing the formation of magnesium oxide from magnesium and oxygen atoms.

b) What name is given to the structure of magnesium oxide?

....

c) Circle the correct words to explain why magnesium oxide has a high melting point.

Magnesium oxide has very **strong** / **weak** chemical bonds between the **negative** / **positive** magnesium ions and the **negative** / **positive** oxygen ions. This means that it takes a **small** / **large** amount of energy to break the bonds and melt the compound.

Q2 Mike conducts an experiment to find out if **sodium chloride** conducts electricity. He tests the compound when it's solid, when it's dissolved in water and when it's molten.

	Conducts electricity?
When solid	
When dissolved in water	
When molten	

a) Complete the table of results opposite.

b) Explain your answers to part a).

....

....

....

Q3 Draw '**dot and cross**' diagrams showing the formation of the following ionic compounds:

a) sodium oxide

b) magnesium chloride

Group 1 — Alkali Metals

Q1   Indicate whether the statements below are **true** or **false**.

		True	False
a)	Alkali metals readily gain electrons to form 1⁺ ions.	☐	☐
b)	Alkali metals form covalent compounds by sharing electrons.	☐	☐
c)	Alkali metals are stored in oil to stop them reacting with oxygen and water in the air.	☐	☐
d)	Alkali metal atoms all have a single electron in their outer shell.	☐	☐
e)	Alkali metals are hard.	☐	☐

Q2   The table shows the **melting points** of some Group 1 metals.

Element	Melting point (°C)
Li	181
Na	98
K	63
Rb	39
Cs	?

a) What is unusual about the **melting points** of the alkali metals compared to other metals?

....

b) Would you expect the melting point of **caesium** to be higher or lower than **rubidium**? Explain your answer.

....

c) Complete the following sentence:

As you move down Group 1, the reactivity of the atoms ....

Q3   Archibald put a piece of **lithium** into a beaker of water.

a) Explain why the lithium floated on top of the water.

....

b) After the reaction had finished, Archibald tested the water with universal indicator. What colour change would he see, and why?

....

....

c) Write a **balanced symbol equation** for the reaction.

....

d) i) Write a word equation for the reaction between rubidium and water.

....

ii) Would you expect the reaction between rubidium and water to be **more** or **less** vigorous than the reaction between lithium and water? Explain your answer.

....

Group 1 — Alkali Metals

Q4   Alkali metal compounds emit characteristic **colours** when heated.

a)   Selina has three powdered samples of alkali metal compounds. Describe an experiment she could carry out to help her identify the alkali metal present.

....

....

....

....

b)   Which **alkali metal** is present in:

i)   an alkali metal nitrate (found in gunpowder) that burns with a lilac flame? ....

ii) a street lamp that emits an orange light? ....

iii) fireworks that produce red flames? ....

Q5   Sodium and potassium are **alkali metals**.

a)   Draw the electronic arrangements of a **sodium atom** and a **potassium atom** in the space provided.

b)   i)   Write a balanced symbol equation to show the formation of a sodium ion from a sodium atom.

....

ii) Is this process oxidation or reduction? Explain your answer.

....

c)   Why do sodium and potassium have similar properties?

....

d)   Why is potassium more reactive than sodium?

....

....

Top Tip: All the alkali metals have a single outer electron, which they're dead keen to get rid of so they have a nice full outer shell. As you move down the group the outer electron gets further away from the nucleus so it's lost more easily — this makes the elements more reactive as you go down the group.

Electrolysis and the Half-Equations

Q1 Draw lines to join the words with their correct meanings.

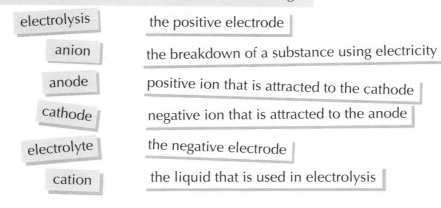

electrolysis — the positive electrode

anion — the breakdown of a substance using electricity

anode — positive ion that is attracted to the cathode

cathode — negative ion that is attracted to the anode

electrolyte — the negative electrode

cation — the liquid that is used in electrolysis

Q2 Explain why the electrolyte needs to be either a **solution** or **molten** for electrolysis to work.

....

....

Q3 The diagram below shows the electrolysis of **sulfuric acid solution**.

a) Identify the ions and molecules labelled A, B, C and D on the diagram.

Choose from the options in the box below.

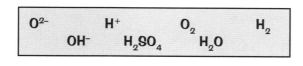

O^{2-} H^+ O_2 H_2
OH^- H_2SO_4 H_2O

A ....   B ....

C ....   D ....

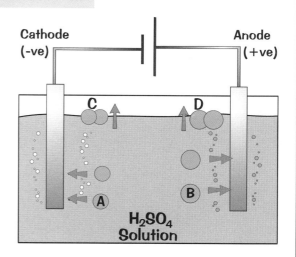

b) Write **balanced** half-equations for the processes that occur during the electrolysis of sulfuric acid solution.

Cathode: ....

Anode: ....

Make sure the charges balance.

c) Why can't pure water be electrolysed?

....

Top Tips: Half-equations just show what's going on at the cathode and anode in terms of electrons — a positive ion gains electrons and a negative ion loses electrons.

Extracting Aluminium

Q1   **Aluminium** is the most **abundant** metal in the Earth's crust.

Goodness, how awfully common... $o_{o_{o_o}}$

a)   i)   Circle the correct word:

The most common aluminium ore is bauxite / cryolite.

ii)   When this ore is mined and purified, which compound is obtained?
Give its name and formula.

Name ....   **Formula** ....

b)   Why can't aluminium be extracted by **reduction** with carbon?

....

c)   Although it's very common, aluminium was not discovered until 1825. Suggest why.

....

Q2 a)   Indicate whether the following statements are **true** or **false**.

True   False

i)   Ionic substances can only be electrolysed if molten or in solution.

☐   ☐

ii)   In the extraction of aluminium the electrolyte is molten aluminium metal.

☐   ☐

iii)   Aluminium oxide is dissolved in molten cryolite before electrolysis begins.

☐   ☐

iv)   Copper electrodes are used in the extraction of aluminium by electrolysis.

☐   ☐

v)   Aluminium is formed at the anode.

☐   ☐

b)   Write out a correct version of each false statement.

....

....

....

....

Q3   The extraction of aluminium by electrolysis is a **redox reaction**.

a)   Write balanced half-equations for the reactions at the electrodes.

Cathode: ....

Anode: ....

b)   Use the half-equations to help explain why this process is called a 'redox' reaction.

....

....

Module C3 — The Periodic Table

Extracting Aluminium

Q4   The diagram shows the set-up of the equipment used to **extract** aluminium by **electrolysis**.

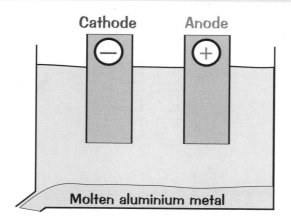

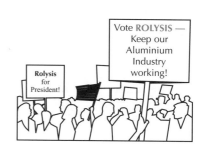

Vote **ROLYSIS** — Keep our Aluminium Industry working!

Rolysis for President!

a)   Why is the aluminium formed as a **liquid**?

....

b)   What substance is formed at the anode? ....

c)   Why does the anode need to be replaced frequently?

....

....

Q5   **Bauxite**, mined in Jamaica, is shipped to Canada to be processed into aluminium because Canada has abundant **hydroelectric power**.

a)   Give three major costs, apart from the mining of the ore, involved in the extraction of aluminium.

   1.   ....

   2.   ....

   3.   ....

b)   Why does it make economic sense to ship the ore to Canada?

....

....

Top Tips: In general, things that are **common** and **easy to get at** are **cheap**. Like potatoes, say. But you can't make drink cans or aeroplane fuselages from potatoes — you need a nice **lightweight metal**, like aluminium. Aluminium is as common a metal as you can get but it's not that cheap because it's expensive to extract — electrolysis costs a lot. (Potatoes, on the other hand, are very easy to extract — you find a **spade** and just get **digging** — no pricey electricity needed.)

Covalent Bonding

Q1 Indicate whether each statement is **true** or **false**.

True False

a) Covalent bonding involves sharing electrons.

b) Atoms react to gain a full outer shell of electrons.

c) Some atoms can make both ionic and covalent bonds.

d) Hydrogen can form two covalent bonds.

e) Carbon can form four covalent bonds.

"Oi, give me that electron big nose!"

Q2 Complete these sentences by circling the correct word from each pair.

a) Substances that contain covalent bonds usually have **giant / simple** molecular structures.

b) Atoms within covalent molecules are held together by **strong / weak** covalent bonds.

c) Intermolecular forces in covalent substances are **strong / weak**. This results in **high / low** melting and boiling points.

d) Molecular substances **do / don't** conduct electricity.

Q3 Complete the following diagrams by adding **electrons**. Only the **outer shells** are shown.

Use • and x to show the electrons from the different elements.

a) Hydrogen (H_2)

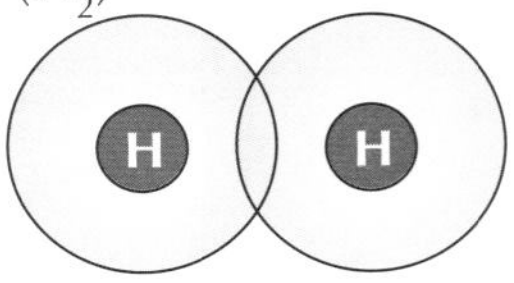

H   H

d) Water (H_2O)

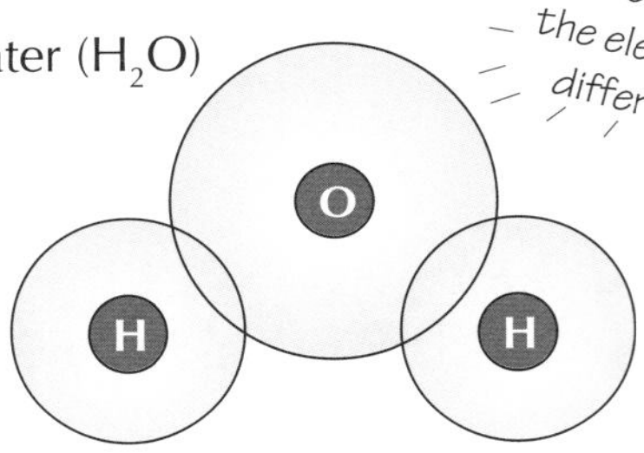

O

H   H

b) Chlorine (Cl_2)

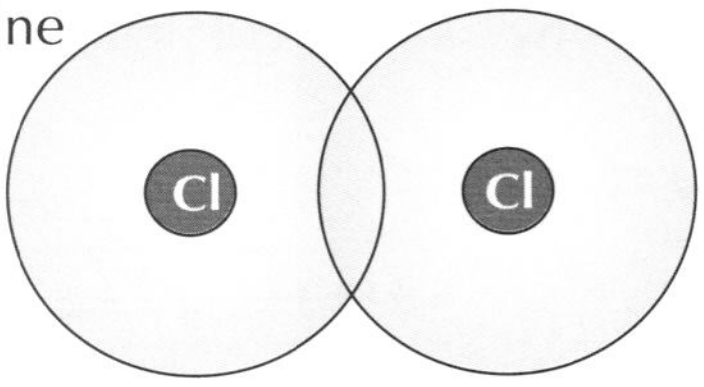

Cl   Cl

e) Methane (CH_4)

H

H   C   H

H

c) Carbon dioxide (CO_2)

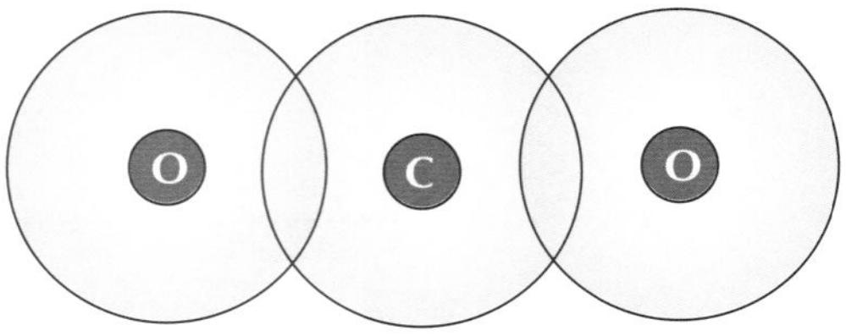

O   C   O

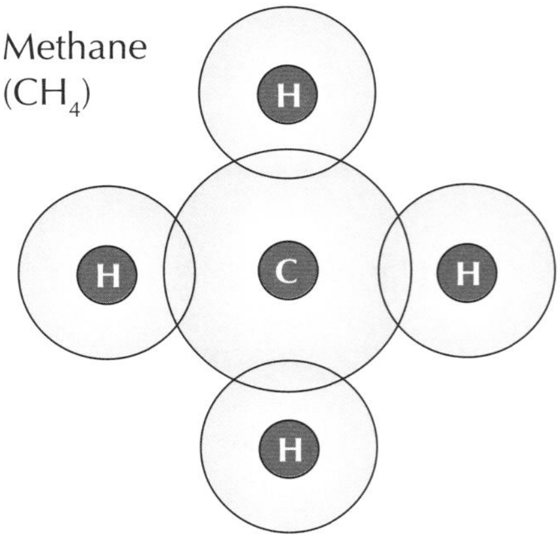

Q4 Explain why chlorine exists as Cl_2 molecules, and not as single atoms.

....

....

Group 7 — Halogens

Q1 Draw lines to match each halogen to its **description**.

chlorine

iodine

bromine

dense green gas

orange liquid

dark grey solid

Hubba hubba

Q2 Tick the correct boxes to say whether these statements are **true** or **false**.

		True	False
a)	Chlorine gas is made up of molecules which each contain three chlorine atoms.	☐	☐
b)	Halogens covalently bond with other non-metals to form molecules.	☐	☐
c)	Chlorine reacts with hydrogen to form an ionic compound.	☐	☐
d)	The halogens become less reactive as you go down the group.	☐	☐
e)	Chlorine and bromine are poisonous.	☐	☐
f)	The halogens readily gain electrons to form 1^+ ions.	☐	☐

Q3 Chlorine and bromine are both **halogens**.

a) Draw the electron arrangements of a **chlorine atom** and a **chloride ion** in the space provided.

b) i) Write a balanced symbol equation to show the formation of chloride ions from a chlorine molecule.

....

ii) Is this process oxidation or reduction? Explain your answer.

....

c) Why do chlorine and bromine have similar properties?

....

d) Why is bromine less reactive than chlorine?

....

Group 7 — Halogens

Q4   **Sodium** was reacted with **bromine vapour** using the equipment shown.
White crystals of a new solid were formed during the reaction.

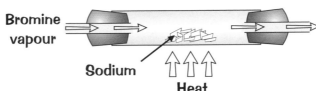

a)   Name the white crystals.

....

b)   Write a balanced symbol equation for the reaction.

....

c)   Would you expect the above reaction to be faster or slower than a similar reaction between:

  i)   sodium and iodine vapour? Explain your answer.

  ....

  ii) sodium and chlorine vapour? Explain your answer.

  ....

Q5   Equal volumes of **bromine water** were added to two test tubes, each containing
a different **potassium halide solution**. The results are shown in the table.

SOLUTION	RESULT
potassium chloride	no colour change
potassium iodide	colour change

a)   Explain these results.

....

....

....

b)   Write a **balanced symbol equation** for the reaction in the potassium iodide solution.

....

c)   Would you expect a reaction between:

  i)   bromine water and potassium astatide? ....

  ii) bromine water and potassium fluoride? ....

Metals

Q1 Draw a diagram in the space below to show the arrangement of the atoms in a typical **metal**. Label the **atoms** and the **free electrons**, and show any relevant charges.

Q2 The table shows the properties of **four elements** found in the periodic table.

ELEMENT	MELTING POINT (°C)	DENSITY (g/cm³)	ELECTRICAL CONDUCTIVITY
A	1084	8.9	Excellent
B	–39	13.6	Very good
C	3500	3.51	Very poor
D	1536	7.87	Very good

a) Which three of the above elements are most likely to be **metals**?

....

b) Explain how you know the other element is **not** a metal.

....

....

c) Suggest the name of **element B** and explain your answer.

....

....

Q3 Explain how **electricity** is conducted through metals.

....

....

Metals

Q4 Complete the following sentences by choosing from the words in the box.

Each word should only be used once.

hammered	weak	low	high	strong	malleable	folded

a) Metals have a .... tensile strength.

b) Metals are .... and hard to break.

c) Metals can be .... into different shapes because they are ....

Q5 Explain why most metals have **high melting points**.

....

....

Q6 **Metals** are used for different things depending on their **properties**.

For each of the uses below, choose the most suitable metal from the list and state one property of the metal that makes it suitable for this purpose.

stainless steel   copper   aluminium   steel

a) Structures like bridges.

Metal   ....

Property   ....

b) Aeroplanes.

Metal   ....

Property   ....

c) Cutlery.

Metal   ....

Property   ....

d) Electrical wiring.

Metal   ....

Property   ....

Top Tip: Okay, so metals form weird bonds. How come the electrons can go wandering about like that? Well actually, that's just the kind of question you **don't** need to ask yourself right now. Don't stress about it, just learn the key phrases examiners like — '**giant structure**', '**sea of free electrons**,' etc.

Superconductors and Transition Metals

Q1   Draw lines to match the transition metal to the process it catalyses.

iron   converting natural oils into fats

nickel   ammonia production

Q2   Complete the passage below by circling the correct word(s) from each pair.

Most metals are in the transition block found **at the left** / **in the middle** of the periodic table.
They generally have high **densities** / **volatility**, **low** / **high** melting points and are **good** / **poor**
conductors of heat and electricity. Their compounds are **colourful** / **shiny** and, like the metals
themselves, are often effective **fuels** / **catalysts**.

Q3   Under normal conditions **all** metals have **electrical resistance**.

a)   Describe how electrical resistance causes energy to be wasted.

....

....

b)   What is a superconductor? ....

c)   Give three possible uses of superconducting wires.

1. ....

2. ....

3. ....

d)   Explain a drawback of using today's superconductors.

....

....

Q4   'Colourful chemical gardens' can be made by sprinkling
transition metal salts into **sodium silicate solution**.
Transition metal silicate crystals grow upwards as shown.

sodium silicate
solution

transition
metal silicates

a)   Why do you think transition metal salts are used?

....

b)   Suggest three colours that you would be likely to see in the garden if iron(II) sulfate,
iron(III) chloride and copper(II) sulfate salts are used.

....

Thermal Decomposition and Precipitation

Q1   Draw lines to match the type of reaction with its description.

> thermal decomposition

> when a substance breaks down into simpler substances when heated

> precipitation

> where two solutions react and an insoluble solid is formed

Q2   Neil heats some **green** copper carbonate, $CuCO_3$. He is left with a **black** solid.

a)   How can Neil tell that a reaction has taken place?

....

b)   What type of reaction has taken place? ....

c)   Write a word equation for this reaction.

....

d)   Describe how you could **test** for **carbon dioxide**.

....

....

Q3   Write **balanced symbol equations** for the thermal decomposition of the following substances.

a)   zinc carbonate, $ZnCO_3$

....

b)   iron(II) carbonate, $FeCO_3$

....

c)   copper(II) carbonate, $CuCO_3$

....

d)   manganese(II) carbonate, $MnCO_3$

....

Thermal Decomposition and Precipitation

Q4
Clear, blue **copper(II) sulfate solution** and clear, colourless **sodium hydroxide** solution were mixed. The liquid went cloudy and pale blue. After a while a **pale blue solid** was left at the bottom and the liquid was **clear** again.

a) What type of reaction has occurred? ....

b) Name the blue solid formed.

....

c) Write a balanced symbol equation for this reaction.

....

d) Write a symbol equation to show the formation of the pale blue solid.

....

Q5
Cilla adds a few drops of **NaOH** solution to solutions of different **metal compounds**.

a) Complete her table of results.

Compound	Metal Cation	Colour of Precipitate
copper(II) sulfate		blue
iron(II) sulfate		
iron(III) chloride	Fe^{3+}	
copper(II) chloride		

b) Write a balanced symbol equation for the reaction of copper(II) chloride with sodium hydroxide.

....

c) Complete the balanced ionic equation for the reaction of iron(II) ions with hydroxide ions.

These ionic equations should only show the ions involved in the formation of the precipitate.

Fe^{2+} + ... OH^- → ....

d) Write a balanced ionic equation for the reaction of **iron(III) ions** with hydroxide ions.

....

e) Explain how this type of reaction could be used to help identify unknown metal ions.

....

....

....

<u>Mixed Questions — Module C3</u>

Q1 Hydrogen atoms can exist as three **isotopes** — ^{1}H (hydrogen), ^{2}H (deuterium) and ^{3}H (tritium).

a) What is an isotope?

....

b) Complete the table.

isotope	number of protons	number of neutrons	number of electrons
^{1}H			
^{2}H			
^{3}H			

c) The atomic number is often left out of the isotope symbol.
For instance, it is acceptable to write ^{12}**C** for carbon-12 rather than $^{12}_{6}$**C**.

i) Define the term **atomic number**.

....

ii) Explain why the atomic number can be left out of the isotope symbol.

....

Q2 **Lithium** is a metallic element in **Group 1** of the periodic table.

a) Draw a diagram to show the electronic arrangement in a lithium atom.

Use the periodic table to help you.

b) Explain how lithium ions usually form.

....

c) **Fluorine** is in **Group 7** of the periodic table. Its electronic arrangement is shown below.

i) Draw a diagram to show the electronic arrangement in a fluoride **ion**.

ii) Give the chemical formula for the compound that forms between lithium and fluorine.

....

iii) What type of bonding is involved in this compound?

....

Module C3 — The Periodic Table

Mixed Questions — Module C3

Q3 The table below gives some data for five **elements**.

Element	Melting point (°C)	Density (g/cm³)	Conducts electricity as solid?	Oxide of element	
				Colour (at RTP)	State (at RTP)
A	1455	8.9	Yes	Green	Solid
B	44	1.82	No	White	Solid
C	3550	3.51	No	Colourless	Gas
D	1535	7.86	Yes	Red	Solid
E	98	0.97	Yes	White	Solid

a) Two of the elements are transition elements. Identify them and explain your answer.

....

....

b) Give a use for one named transition element.

Transistion element: .... Use: ....

Q4 **Aluminium** is extracted from its ore by **electrolysis**.

a) What is electrolysis?

....

b) The aluminium ions are attracted to the negative cathode.

i) Explain what happens to the aluminium ions at the cathode.

....

ii) Complete a balanced half-equation for the reaction that takes place.

Al^{3+} + ... → ....

c) Oxygen ions are attracted to the anode.
Complete a balanced half-equation for the reaction there.

$2O^{2-}$ → .... + ...

d) Electrolysis is a redox reaction. Explain what this means.

....

e) In order to electrolyse aluminium oxide, it is dissolved in molten cryolite.
Explain why this is more cost-effective than just melting the aluminium oxide.

....

....

Mixed Questions — Module C3

Q5   The diagram shows the apparatus used to react **chlorine** with **magnesium**.

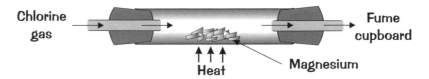

Chlorine gas → ... Fume cupboard

↑ ↑ ↑ Heat   Magnesium

a)   Why is it not possible to use the same apparatus to react iodine with magnesium?

....

b)   Complete the chemical equation for the reaction: **Mg + Cl$_2$ →** ....

c)   What type of bonding is present in the product? ....

d)   Draw a dot and cross diagram to show the formation of magnesium chloride from magnesium and chlorine atoms.

e)   Solid magnesium chloride does not conduct electricity. However, when magnesium chloride is dissolved in water or is molten it does conduct electricity. Explain these facts.

....

....

Q6   Metals are good **electrical conductors**. Explain why, using ideas about structure and bonding.

....

....

....

Q7   Iodine has a **simple molecular structure**.

a)   What type of bonding binds the iodine atoms together in each molecule? ....

b)   Explain why iodine has a low melting point.

....

....

c)   Predict whether iodine is likely to be able to conduct electricity. Justify your prediction.

....

....

Speed and Acceleration

Q1 Ealing is about 12 km west of Marble Arch. It takes a tube train 20 minutes to get to Marble Arch from Ealing.

Circle the letter next to the **true** statement below.

A The average speed of the train is 60 m/s.

B The average speed of the train is 10 m/s.

C The average speed of the train is 60 m/s due east.

D The average speed of the train is 36 m/s.

Albert Square   Marble Arch

Ealing   Walford East

Q2 A pulse of laser light takes 1.3 seconds to travel from the Moon to the Earth.

If the speed of light is 3×10^8 m/s, how far away is the Moon from the Earth in km?

....

....

You'll need to rearrange the speed formula.

Q3 I rode my bike 1500 m to the shops. It took me 5 minutes.

a) What was my average speed in m/s?

....

b) One part of the journey was downhill and I averaged 15 m/s over this 300 m stretch. How long did it take to cover this bit of the journey?

....

c) Going home I took a different route and my average speed was 4 m/s. It took me 8 minutes. How far is the journey home?

....

....

Q4 The speed limit for cars on the motorway is 70 mph (about 31 m/s). A motorist accelerated onto the motorway from a service station and was captured on a speed camera. He denied speeding.

Look at his **distance-time** graph.
Was the motorist telling the truth?

....

....

Think... you need to find the speed from a distance-time graph.

Distance (m)

72
60
48
36
24
12
0

0.5   1.0   1.5   2.0   2.5   3.0

Time (s)

Speed and Acceleration

Q5 Steve walked to football training only to find that he'd left his boots at home. He turned round and walked back home, where he spent 30 seconds looking for them. To make it to training on time he had to run back at twice his walking speed.

Below is an incomplete **distance-time graph** for his journey.

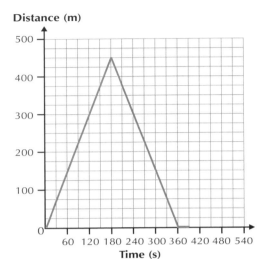

Distance (m)

a) How long did it take Steve to walk to training?

....

b) Calculate Steve's speed for the first section of the graph in m/s.

....

c) Complete the graph to show Steve's run back.

Q6 The graph shows the motion of a train as it travels from Alphaville to Charlietown, where it stops briefly, and then moves off again.

a) Describe the motion of the train in the sections marked:

A ....

B ....

C ....

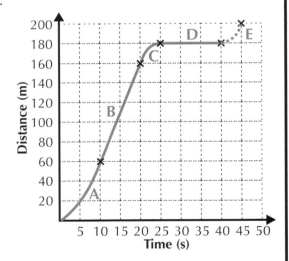

b) What is the train's **average** speed between Alphaville and Charlietown?

....

....

c) Calculate the **maximum** speed of the train between the two stations.

....

d) How long does the train stop at Charlietown?

....

Speed and Acceleration

Q7 The Go Go car company make gas-powered model cars.
One car accelerates from rest to 20 m/s in 3.5 s.

a) What is its acceleration?

....

b) The car is modified and now accelerates from 3 m/s to 20 m/s in 2.8 s.
Show that this modification has improved the car's acceleration.

....

....

Q8 An egg is dropped from the top of the Eiffel tower.
It hits the ground after 8 seconds, at a speed of 80 m/s.

a) Find the egg's acceleration. ....

b) How long did it take for the egg to reach 40 m/s?

....

Q9 A car accelerates at 2 m/s². After 4 seconds it reaches a speed of 24 m/s.

How fast was it going before it started to accelerate?

....

....

Q10 Below is a speed-time graph for the descent of a lunar lander.
It accelerates due to the pull of gravity from the Moon.

Use the graph to calculate this acceleration.

....

....

....

Speed and Acceleration

Q11 The graph on the right shows a speed-skater's performance during a race.

a) How far does the skater go in the following sections:

X? ....

....

Y? ....

....

Z? ....

....

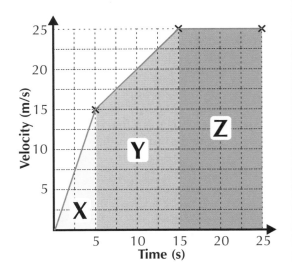

b) If the race finishes after 25 s, how far will she have travelled altogether?

....

Q12 Match each line on the distance-time graph with the correct line on the velocity-time graph.

Distance-Time Graph

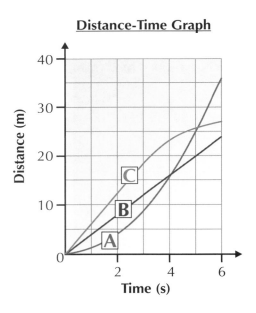

Velocity-Time Graph

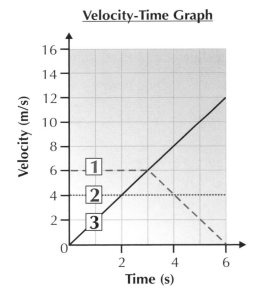

Line **A** = Line ....

Line **B** = Line ....

Line **C** = Line ....

Top Tips:

The most confusing thing about acceleration can be interpreting the graphs. The key thing to remember on a V-T graph is that the steepness of the line is the acceleration. If the line is curved, the acceleration is changing — the steeper the line, the greater the acceleration. Learn these facts and the graphs won't just look like a bunch of lines — they'll look like lines... but with meaning.

Module P3 — Forces for Transport

Forces

Q1   A teapot sits on a table.

a)   Explain why it doesn't sink into the table.

....

b)   Jane picks up the teapot and hangs it from the ceiling by a rope.
What vertical forces now act on the teapot?

....

c)   The rope breaks and the teapot accelerates towards the floor.

i)   Are the vertical forces balanced? ....

ii)   The teapot hits the floor without breaking and bounces upwards.
Which force causes the teapot to bounce upwards?

....

Q2   A bear rides a bike north at a constant speed.

a)   Label the forces acting on the bear.

....

b)   The bear brakes and slows down.
Are the forces balanced **as** he slows
down? If not, which direction is the
overall force in?

....

....

Q3   Khaleeda helps Jenny investigate falling objects. Jenny lets go of
a tennis ball and Khaleeda times how long it takes to fall. Khaleeda
draws the distance-time graph — it looks like the one shown.

Which phrase below describes points X, Y and Z?
Explain what feature of the graph allows you to tell.

forces in balance   **reaction force from ground acts**

unbalanced force of gravity

*What does the gradient of a
distance-time graph tell you?*

X: ....

You can tell this because ....

Y: .... You can tell this because:

....

Z: .... You can tell this because:

....

Friction Forces and Terminal Speed

Q1 Use the words supplied to fill in the blanks in the paragraph below about a sky-diver.

decelerates	decrease	less	balances	increase	constant	greater	accelerates

When a sky-diver jumps out of a plane, his weight is .... than his air resistance, so he .... downwards. This causes his air resistance to .... until it .... his weight. At this point, his velocity is .... When his parachute opens, his air resistance is .... than his weight, so he .... This causes his air resistance to .... until it .... his weight. Then his velocity is .... once again.

Q2 Which of the following will **not** reduce the drag force on an aeroplane?
Tick the appropriate box.

☐ flying higher (where the air is thinner)   ☐ carrying less cargo

☐ flying more slowly   ☐ making the plane more streamlined

Q3 A scientist is investigating gravity by dropping a hammer and a feather.
Comment on the following predictions and explanations of what will happen.

a) "They will land at the same time — gravity is the same for both."

....

....

b) "The feather will reach its terminal velocity before the hammer."

....

....

Q4 You're investigating drag by dropping balls into a measuring cylinder full of oil and timing how long they take to reach the bottom. You have a golf ball, a glass marble and a ball bearing.

From this experiment, can you make any conclusions about the effect of size on drag?
Explain your answer.

....

....

....

Friction Forces and Terminal Speed

Q5   Explain what is meant when an object is described as streamlined.

....

....

Q6   Simon wants to test different lubricants by sliding a heavy block across a board covered in different substances. He measures how much force is required to get the block moving.

Surface substance	Force needed to get block moving (N)
Banana skins	40
Grease	36
Oil	30
Water	38

a)   **i)**   What is the maximum value of the static friction for water?

....

ii)   Suggest why oil is used as a lubricant.

....

b)   Simon does a similar experiment with a toy boat in a swimming pool.
He measures the force required to keep the boat moving at different speeds.

To keep the boat moving at a higher speed, what would need to happen to the force?

....

Q7   The graph shows how the velocity of a sky-diver changes before and after he opens his parachute.

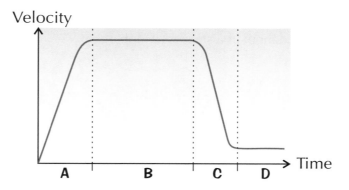

For each of the four regions A-D say whether the force of **weight** or **air resistance** is greater, or if they are **equal**.

Region A: ....   Region B: ....

Region C: ....   Region D: ....

Forces and Acceleration

Q1   Use the words supplied to fill in the blanks. You may need to use some words more than once.

proportional	force	reaction	stationary	accelerates	opposite
	constant	resultant	inversely	balanced	

If the forces on an object are .... , it's either .... or

moving at .... speed.

If an object has a .... force acting on it, it .... in the

direction of the .... The acceleration is .... to the force

and .... to its mass.

For every action there is an equal and ....·

Q2   You're travelling home from school on a bus doing a steady speed in a straight line.
Which of the following is true? Tick the appropriate box.

☐ The driving force of the engine is bigger than friction and air resistance combined.

☐ There are no forces acting on the bus.

☐ The driving force of the engine is equal to friction and air resistance combined.

☐ No force is required to keep the bus moving.

Q3   State whether or not the forces acting on the following items are **balanced**,
and explain your reasoning.

a)   A cricket ball slowing down as it rolls along the outfield.

....

b)   A car going round a roundabout at a steady 30 mph.

....

c)   A vase knocked off a window ledge.

....

d)   A satellite orbiting over a fixed point on the Earth's surface.

....

e)   A bag of rubbish ejected from a spacecraft in deep space.

....

Forces and Acceleration

Q4 Put these cars in order of increasing driving force.

Car	Mass (kg)	Maximum acceleration (m/s²)
Disraeli 9000	800	5
Palmerston 6i	1560	0.7
Heath TT	950	3
Asquith 380	790	2

1. ....

2. ....

3. ....

4. ....

Q5 Jo and Brian have fitted both their scooters with the same engine. Brian and his scooter have a combined mass of 110 kg and an acceleration of 2.80 m/s². On her scooter, Jo only manages an acceleration of 1.71 m/s².

a) What **force** can the engine exert?

....

b) Calculate the combined mass of Jo and her scooter.

....

Q6 Tom drags a 1 kg mass along a table with a newton-meter so that it accelerates at 0.25 m/s². If the newton-meter reads 0.4 N, what's the force of friction between the mass and the table?

....

....

Q7 A car tows a caravan along a road. At a constant speed, the pulling force of the car and the opposing reaction force of the caravan are equal. Which statement correctly describes the forces between the caravan and the car when the car accelerates? Tick the appropriate box.

☐ "The caravan's reaction force cancels out the pulling force of the car, so the caravan won't accelerate."

☐ "The caravan's reaction force is at a right angle to the force pulling the car, so the two forces don't affect one another."

☐ "The car's pulling force accelerates the caravan. The caravan's reaction acts on the car, not the caravan."

Q8 Which picture shows the weight (w) and reaction force (R) of a car on a slope? Tick the appropriate box.

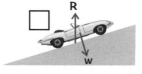 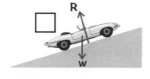 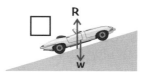 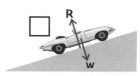

Forces and Acceleration

Q9 Which of the following statements correctly explains what happens when you walk?
Tick the appropriate box.

☐ Your feet push backwards on the ground, so the ground pushes you forwards.

☐ The force in your muscles overcomes the friction between your feet and the ground.

☐ The ground's reaction can't push you backwards because of friction.

☐ Your feet push forwards, and the ground's reaction is upwards.

Q10 A camper van with a mass of 2500 kg has a maximum driving force of 2650 N. It is
driven along a straight, level road at a constant speed of 90 kilometres per hour. At this
speed, air resistance is 2000 N and the friction between the tyres and the road is 500 N.

a) **i)** What force is the engine exerting? ....

ii) Complete the diagram to show all the forces acting on the camper van.
Give the size of each force.

b) A strong headwind begins blowing, with a force of **200 N**. The van slows down.
Calculate its deceleration.

....

c) The driver notices that the van is slowing and puts his foot right down on the accelerator,
applying the maximum driving force. How does the acceleration of the camper van change?
(Assume that air resistance and friction remain at their previous values.)

....

....

....

Top Tips:
A resultant force means your object will accelerate — it will change its speed or
direction (or both). But if your object has a constant speed (which could be zero) and a constant
direction, you can say with utter confidence that there ain't any resultant force. Be careful though —
a zero resultant force doesn't mean there are **no** forces, just that they all balance each other out.

Stopping Distances

Q1 A car driver's reaction time is 0.7 s. How far will the car go before the brakes are applied in an emergency, if it is travelling at 20 m/s? Tick the box next to the correct answer.

☐ 0.7 m   ☐ 14 m   ☐ 20 m   ☐ 28.6 m

Q2 The distance a car takes to stop is divided into: i) thinking distance and ii) braking distance.

a) Explain what the thinking distance is for a driver.

....

b) Why does a tired driver have a greater thinking distance?

....

Q3 Indicate whether the following statements are **true** or **false**.

		True	False
a)	Tyres have a tread so they grip onto the water in wet weather.	☺	☹
b)	The braking distance will be the same for all road surfaces.	☺	☹
c)	The more heavily a car is loaded, the shorter its stopping distance.	☺	☹
d)	The minimum legal tyre tread depth is 1.6 mm.	☺	☹
e)	The total stopping distance is the thinking distance + the braking distance.	☺	☹

Q4 Tyres should have a minimum tread depth to stop the car **aquaplaning** in wet conditions. What is "aquaplaning" and why is it **unsafe**?

....

....

Q5 A car is travelling along a dry country road at **90 km/h**. The driver sees a stop sign ahead of him and brakes. His thinking time is **0.6 s**.

You need to sort out the units first for all of these questions.

a) Work out his **thinking distance**.

....

b) Once the driver hits the brakes the car decelerates at a constant rate and takes 3.8 s to come to a stop.

i) Calculate the car's **average speed** (in m/s) during its deceleration.

....

ii) Use your answer to part i) to help you calculate the car's **braking distance** .

....

Car Safety

Q1 A car travels along a level road and brakes to avoid hitting a cat.

a) What type of **energy** does the moving car have?

....

b) Explain how energy is **conserved** as the brakes slow down the car.

....

Q2 Use the words supplied to fill in the blanks in the passage below.

crashes	safety	power	interact	control

Many modern cars have active .... features. These ....

with the way the car is driven to help avoid .... These features

include .... -assisted steering and traction ....

Q3 The graph below shows the number of people killed in motorway traffic accidents in the country of Thornland.

a) What is the overall trend shown by the graph?

....

b) Suggest a possible reason for this trend.

....

....

Q4 Modern cars are now fitted with many **safety features**.

a) Why are car safety features designed to **slow** the car and its occupants down over the **longest** possible time in a collision?

....

....

b) State **two** safety features which increase the time taken for passengers to slow down in a crash. For each feature, explain **how** it helps to convert kinetic energy more safely.

....

....

....

Car Safety

Q5   Since 1991 it has been compulsory in the UK for all adults
to wear seat belts in both the front and back seats of a car.

a)   Explain how a seat belt **absorbs** energy to slow down a passenger when a crash occurs.

....

b)   Why do seat belts have to be replaced after a crash? ....

....

Q6   A **safety cage** is a safety feature in a car.

a)   Is it a **passive** or an **active** safety feature? ....

b)   How does it keep the occupants safe?

....

....

Q7   Explain how **crash barriers** on roads can keep passengers safer in a collision.

....

....

Q8   Explain how the following features make driving a car safer.

a)   Adjustable seats.

....

b)   Control paddles near the steering wheel, e.g. stereo controls.

Control
Paddle

....

....

Q9   Two identical cars drive at the same speed down a dry road. One car is fitted with **ABS brakes**.
Both cars brake heavily at the same time. The car without ABS skids before coming to a halt.

a)   Are ABS brakes an **active** or a **passive** safety feature? ....

b)   Which car would you expect to have the shorter braking distance?
Explain your answer in terms of **friction**.

....

....

Work and Potential Energy

Q1   Jenny kicks a football, giving it **50 J** of energy.

   a)   How much work does Jenny do?

   ....

   b)   If Jenny kicks the ball with a force of **250 N**, over what **distance** does her kick act on the ball?

   ....

Q2   Explain why pushing your bicycle along a **level** road
          means that you do some **work** in the scientific sense.

   ....

   ....

Q3   Indicate whether the following statements are **true** or **false**.

		True	False
a)	Potential energy = mass × g × height.	☺	☹
b)	Work done is the energy possessed by an object due to height.	☺	☹
c)	On Earth, the gravitational field strength is approximately **10 N/kg**.	☺	☹
d)	When a force moves an object, work is done.	☺	☹
e)	On Earth, a **3 kg** chicken flies up 2.5 m to sit on a fence. It gains about **75 J** of gravitational potential energy.	☺	☹

Q4   Dave works at a DIY shop. He has to load **28** flagstones onto the delivery truck.
          Each flagstone has a mass of **25 kg** and has to be lifted **1.2 m** onto the truck.

   a)   How much gravitational potential energy does one flagstone
            gain when lifted onto the truck? (g = 10 N/kg)

   ....

   b)   What is the **total gravitational potential energy** gained by the flagstones after they are all loaded
            onto the truck?

   ....

   c)   How much **work** does Dave do loading the truck?

   ....

   ....

Module P3 — Forces for Transport

Work and Potential Energy

Q5   Shelagh keeps fit by cycling every day. She's calculated that she applies a **steady force** of **50 N** as she cycles. She decides to do at least **80 kJ** of work at each session.

a)   What is the minimum distance Shelagh needs to cycle each session?

....

b)   Shelagh says "For every 80 kJ of work I do moving the bike, I must be using up exactly 80 kJ of energy from my food." Is she right? Explain your answer.

....

Q6   Jo is sitting at the top of a helter-skelter ride and her mass is **50 kg**.

a)   If her gravitational potential energy is **4000 J**, how high up is Jo?

$g = 10$ N/kg

....

b)   She comes down the helter-skelter and at the bottom her kinetic energy is **1500 J**. How much **energy** has been 'wasted' coming down the ride?

....

c)   Which **force** causes this energy to be wasted? ....

d)   If the ride is **50 m** long, what is the average energy-wasting force?

....

e)   Jo has another go on the helter-skelter but this time she slides down on a mat. At the bottom of the ride, her kinetic energy is **2000 J**. What is the average energy-wasting **force** on this turn on the ride?

....

....

f)   Explain why Jo has a **different** kinetic energy at the bottom when she slides down on a mat.

....

g)   At the bottom of the ride Jo and the mat take a distance of **5 m** to stop. What is the average stopping **force**?

....

....

5 m

Top Tips:

The main thing to remember is that **energy transferred** and **work done** are just the **same** thing. You're bound to get asked to do a calculation, so make sure you know the couple of equations and how to use them. All work questions are pretty similar — so just keep practising and you'll be fine.

Kinetic Energy

Q1   A car of mass **1000 kg** travels at **10 m/s**.

a)   What is its **kinetic energy**?

....

b)   Decide if the following statements are **true** or **false**.

	True	False

Kinetic energy is energy due to movement.

If a driver doubles her speed, her braking distance will be twice as far.

If the mass of a car is doubled, the braking distance will double.

Brakes convert kinetic energy into mostly heat energy to slow down a car.

Q2   A toy cricket ball hit straight upwards has a gravitational potential energy of **242 J** at the **top** of its flight.

a)   What is the ball's **kinetic energy just** before it hits the ground?

....

b)   Calculate the speed of the ball at this time if its mass is **100 g**.

....

Q3   A large truck and a car both have a kinetic energy of **614 400 J**. The mass of the truck is **12 288 kg** and the car **1200 kg**.

a)   Calculate the **speed** of:

i)   the car ....

ii)   the truck ....

b)   John is playing with his remote-controlled toy car and truck. The car's mass is 100 g. The truck's mass is 300 g. The car is moving twice as fast as the truck. Which has more kinetic energy — the car or the truck? Explain your answer.

....

Q4   Jack rides his bicycle along a level road and has a total kinetic energy of **1440 J**. He brakes, exerting a force of **200 N** on the wheels. How far does he travel before he stops?

....

Top Tips: It's all about moving — the bigger the mass and the faster something moves the larger its kinetic energy. Get friendly with that formula — it crops up everywhere, especially in questions on energy conservation and work. It's not that bad really, so get learning.

Gravity and Roller Coasters

Q1 An astronaut goes to Mars to do some experiments.

Woohoo!
Who needs diets?
Just go to Mars...

a) Explain why her **mass** stays the same but her **weight** changes.

....

b) She takes a rock that weighs **50 N** on Earth. Using a set of scales designed
for use on Earth, she finds that the mass of the rock appears to be **1.9 kg** on Mars.
Calculate the **acceleration due to gravity** on Mars.

....

Q2 A roller coaster and passengers are stationary at the top of a ride.
At this point they have a gravitational potential energy of **300 kJ**.

a) Draw lines to connect the correct energy statement with each stage of the roller coaster.

A
B
C
D

minimum P.E., maximum K.E.

K.E. is being converted to P.E.

maximum P.E.

P.E. is being converted to K.E.

K.E. = Kinetic energy
P.E. = gravitational
potential energy

b) i) When the roller coaster is at half its original height, how much **kinetic energy** should it have?

....

ii) Explain why in real life the kinetic energy is **less** than this.

....

Q3 The planet Greldar has a large roller coaster.

a) If **g = 15 N/kg** on Greldar, calculate the **weight** of a full train if its mass is **1500 kg**.

....

b) At the start of the ride, the roller coaster rises up to its highest point of **25 m**.

i) What is its gain in gravitational **potential energy**?

....

ii) How much **work** does the motor need to do to get the roller coaster to the top of the ride?

....

Power

Q1   Complete this passage by using the words provided.

heat	energy	one hundred	rate	light	watts	joules

Power is the .... of doing work, or how much .... is

transferred per second. It is measured in .... or .... per

second.

A 100 W light bulb transfers .... joules of electrical energy into

.... and .... each second.

Q2   George drives to work every day in a small car with a **power** output of **50 kW**.

a)   Write down an equation that relates **power** to **energy**.

....

b)   If the journey takes **5 minutes**, how much **energy** does the car get from its fuel?

....

c)   One day George's car breaks down and so he cycles to work. The journey takes him
12 minutes and he uses **144 kJ** of energy. How much **power** does he generate?

....

Q3   Catherine and Sally decide to run up a set of stairs to see who can get to the
top more quickly. Catherine has a mass of **46 kg** and Sally has a mass of **48 kg**.

$g = 10$ N/kg

a)   The top of the stairs is **5 m** above ground.
Calculate the gain in **potential energy** for:

i)   Catherine

....

46 kg

48 kg

5 m

ii) Sally

....

b)   Catherine won the race in **6.2 s**, while Sally took **6.4 s**.
Which girl generated more **power**?

....

....

Power

Q4 Tom likes to build model boats. His favourite boat is the Carter, which has a motor power of **150 W**.

a) How much **energy** does the Carter transfer in **10 minutes**?

....

b) The petrol for the boat's motor can supply **30 kJ/ml**.
What volume of petrol is used up in **10 minutes**?

....

c) Tom decides to get a model speed boat which transfers **120 kJ** in the same 10 minute journey. What is the **power** of the engine?

....

Q5 Josie runs home after school so she can watch her favourite TV programme. She has a mass of **60 kg** and her school bag has a mass of **6 kg**.

a) At the start of her run, she accelerates steadily from **0** to **8 m/s** in **6 seconds** while carrying her bag. Calculate her power for this part of her run.

....

b) Josie gets to her house, she puts **down** her school bag, and then runs up the stairs to her room. It takes her **4 seconds** to get to the top of the stairs, where she is **5 m** above ground level. How much power does she generate getting up the stairs?

....

Q6 Andy loves running and wants to improve his starts in sprint races. He uses a timing gate to measure his maximum speed and how long the start takes him. He has a mass of **70 kg**.

Sprint number	Time taken (s)	Maximum speed (m/s)
1	3.2	8.0
2	3.1	8.2
3	3.3	7.9
4 *	4.6	7.2
5	3.2	7.9

*He slips at the start because his shoes don't grip properly.

a) Andy records data for five starts as shown. Information for which start should be ignored?

....

b) Calculate the average **time** taken and the average **speed** achieved in the reliable starts.

....

....

c) What is Andy's average **power** over the reliable starts?

....

Module P3 — Forces for Transport

Fuels for Cars

Q1 Petrol is made from oil, which is a **fossil fuel**.

a) Are fossil fuels **renewable** or **non-renewable**? ....

b) Give **two** environmental problems that burning fossil fuels in cars can cause.

1. ....

2. ....

c) Give an example of an 'alternative fuel' to petrol and diesel. ....

Q2 Trevor's car has two engines, a normal **petrol engine** and an **electric motor**. He uses the electric motor for short journeys but uses the petrol engine for longer drives.

a) How does using the electric motor cause less damage to the **environment**?

....

b) Explain why Trevor has to use the petrol engine for **longer** journeys.

....

c) The electric motor is powered by batteries that need to be frequently charged from a mains supply. If Trevor always used the electric motor, would his driving have any impact on the environment? Explain your answer.

....

....

Q3 A car's fuel consumption is **3.4 l/100 km**. How much fuel is used in a **250 km** journey? Tick the correct box.

☐ 3.4 l ☐ 8.5 l ☐ 6.8 l ☐ 10.0 l

Q4 The fuel consumption of a car can **vary**.

a) State and explain why the following will **increase** or **decrease** the fuel consumption of a moving car.

i) Roof racks ....

....

ii) Open windows ....

....

b) How does fuel consumption vary with the **speed** of a car?

....

Mixed Questions — Module P3

Q1 Mr Alonso drives his car at a constant speed for **1500 m**. The engine produces a force of **300 N**.

a) How much work does the engine do?

....

b) Mr Alonso then accelerates, increasing his speed by 20 m/s over 6.2 s. Calculate his acceleration.

....

c) As it's a hot day, Mr Alonso winds down his windows.
Explain how and why this will alter the **fuel consumption** of the car.

....

....

d) Explain how wearing a seat belt will keep Mr Alonso safer in a crash.

....

....

Q2 Jack and Jill go up a hill to go on a roller coaster. With them
in it, the roller coaster carriage has a total mass of **1200 kg**.

a) What is the weight of the carriage? (Assume g = 10 m/s^2.) ....

b) At the start of the ride the carriage rises up to its highest point of **34 m** above the ground
and stops. Calculate its gain in potential energy.

....

c) The carriage then falls to a third of its maximum height. Assuming there is no air resistance or
friction, calculate the speed of the carriage at this point.

....

....

....

d) At the end of the ride, the carriage slows down, decelerating at **6.4 m/s^2**.
How long does it take the carriage to slow down from 20 m/s and come to a stop?

....

....

Mixed Questions — Module P3

Q3   Norman loves trainspotting. As a special treat, he not only notes
the train numbers but plots a **distance-time** graph for two of the trains.

a)   For how long is train 2 stationary?

....

b)   Both trains start at a steady speed.
How do we know this?

....

c)   Calculate the initial speed of the faster train.

....

d)   Describe the motion of train 1 between 40 s and 80 s.

....

Q4   Cherie robs a bank and escapes in a getaway car with a mass of **2100 kg**.
She travels at a constant speed of **90 km/h** along a straight, level road.

a)   Calculate the kinetic energy of the car.

....

b)   Is there a resultant force on the car? Explain your answer.

....

c)   A police car swings into the middle of the road and stops ahead of Cherie's car. Cherie brakes
with a reaction time of **0.7 s** and a braking time of **3.2 s**.

i)   Calculate her thinking distance.

....

ii)   What happens to the kinetic energy of the car as Cherie slows down?

....

d)   The getaway car has ABS brakes.

i)   Are ABS brakes an active or passive safety feature? ....

ii)   How would you expect having ABS brakes to influence Cherie's braking distance?

....

Module P3 — Forces for Transport

Mixed Questions — Module P3

Q5   In the film 'Crouching Sparrow, Hidden Beaver', a **95 kg** dummy is
dropped **60 m** from the top of a building. (Assume that g = 10 m/s².)

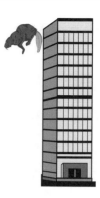

a)   Sketch a distance-time graph and a velocity-time graph for the dummy
from the moment it is dropped until just after it hits the ground.
(Ignore air resistance and assume the dummy does not reach a terminal speed.)

b)   Do any forces act on the dummy when it lies still on the ground (after falling)? If so, what are they?

....

c)   The take doesn't go to plan so the dummy is lifted back to the top of the building using a motor.

    i)   How much work is done on the dummy to get it to the top of the building?

....

    ii)   The useful power output of the motor is **760 W**.
How long does it take to get the dummy to the top of the building?

....

Q6   A sky-diver jumps out of an aeroplane.
Her weight is **700 N**.

a)   What force causes her to accelerate downwards?

....

b)   After **10 s** she is falling at a steady speed of **60 m/s**.
State the force of air resistance that is acting on her.

....

c)   She now opens her parachute, which increases the air resistance to **2000 N**.
Explain what happens immediately after she opens the parachute.

....

....

d)   After falling with her parachute open for **5 s**, the sky-diver is travelling at a steady speed of **4 m/s**.
What is the air resistance force now?

....

Module P3 — Forces for Transport

Leaf Structure

Q1   Write the word equation for **photosynthesis**.

....

Q2   Name the parts labelled **A – E** to complete the diagram of a **leaf** below.

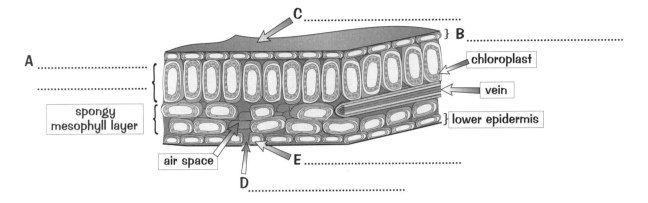

Q3   Look at the diagram on the right and answer the questions below.

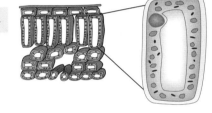

a)   What type of cell is this?

....

b)   What is the function of this cell?

....

c)   Give **two** ways that this cell is adapted for its function.

....

Q4   Draw lines to match up the following **features** of a leaf with how they help with **photosynthesis**.

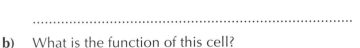

air spaces in mesophyll layer   short diffusion distance

broad leaves   deliver water and nutrients to leaf cells

veins   large surface area exposed to light

thin leaves   large surface area for gas exchange

Q5   Circle the correct word in each pair to complete the passage below.

Stomata are tiny holes found mainly on the **upper / lower** surface of the leaf. They allow carbon dioxide to diffuse **in / out** and oxygen to diffuse **in / out** of the leaf during photosynthesis. The stomata also allow water to **leave / enter** the leaf — this water **loss / gain** is called **transcription / transpiration**.

Diffusion in Leaves

Q1 Tick the box next to the correct definition of **diffusion**.

☐ Diffusion is a process which **requires energy** and involves the movement of particles from an area of **higher** concentration to an area of **lower** concentration.

☐ Diffusion is a process which **does not require energy** and involves the movement of particles from an area of **lower** concentration to an area of **higher** concentration.

☐ Diffusion is a process which **does not require energy** and involves the movement of particles from an area of **higher** concentration to an area of **lower** concentration.

Q2 The diagram shows a leaf which is **photosynthesising**.

a) On the diagram which arrows show the net movement of **oxygen**?

............, ... and ....

b) On the diagram which arrows show the net movement of **carbon dioxide**?

............, ... and ....

c) Add an arrow labelled **X** to show the net movement of **water vapour**.

Q3 Answer the following questions about **gas exchange** in leaves.

a) Which process in the leaf uses CO_2 and produces O_2? ....

b) Which process in the leaf uses O_2 and produces CO_2? ....

Q4 Complete the table by putting ticks in the correct boxes to show if each process happens during the **day**, during the **night**, or **both**.

Process	Day	Night
Photosynthesis		
Respiration		
CO_2 diffuses in		
O_2 diffuses in		

Osmosis

Q1   Look at the diagram and answer the questions below.

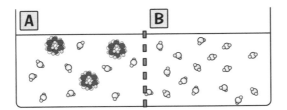
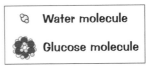

a)   On which side of the membrane is there the highest concentration of water molecules? ....

b)   Predict whether the level of liquid on side B will **rise** or **fall**. Explain your answer.

The liquid level on side B will ...., because ....

....

Q2   A **red blood cell** is in some very **dilute** blood plasma.

Learning by osmosis

a)   Will water move into or out of the cell? Explain your answer.

....

....

b)   Describe what will eventually happen to the cell, and give the technical term for it.

....

c) i)   Describe what happens to an animal cell if it **takes in** too much water.

....

ii)   Describe what happens to an animal cell if it **loses** too much water.

....

Q3 a)   Fill in the missing words to complete the paragraph.

Osmosis is the movement of .... molecules across a

.... permeable .... from a region of

.... water concentration to a region of .... water

concentration. Osmosis is a special type of ....

b)   How is osmosis different from diffusion?

....

....

Osmosis

Q4 Some **potato cylinders** were placed in solutions of different **salt concentrations**. At the start of the experiment each cylinder was 50 mm long. Their final lengths are recorded in the table below.

Concentration of salt solution (molar)	Length of potato cylinder (mm)	Change in length of potato cylinder (mm)
0	60	
0.5	56	
1	50	
1.5	34	
2.0	45	

a) Plot a bar chart showing salt concentration and the final length of the potato cylinders.

b) Work out the change in length of each of the cylinders and write your answers in the table above.

c) Study the pattern of the results.

   i) State the salt concentration(s) that produced unexpected results. ....

   ii) Suggest a method for making the results more reliable.

   ....

d) State **three** factors that should have remained constant to ensure that this was a fair test.

....

....

Q5 Plant cells look different depending on how much **water** they contain.

a) Use the words in the box below to describe the states of the following cells.

plasmolysed	turgid	normal	flaccid

A ....   B ....   C ....   D ....

b) Explain why plants start to wilt if they don't have enough water.

....

....

c) Explain why the cell in diagram D hasn't totally lost its shape.

....

Water Flow Through Plants

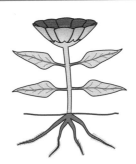

Q1   Complete this diagram of a **plant** according to the instructions given below.

   a)   Put an **X** on the diagram to show one place where water enters the plant.

   b)   Add a **Y** to the diagram to show one place where water leaves the plant.

   c)   Add arrows to the diagram to show how water moves from where
it enters to where it leaves.

Q2   **Root hair cells** are found on the roots of plants.

   a)   Draw a diagram of a root hair cell in the box provided.

   b)   Describe how water is drawn into this cell.

   ....

   ....

Q3   The diagram shows an **open stoma** and a **closed stoma**.

   a)   Label the following: **open stoma**,   **flaccid guard cell**,   **turgid guard cell**,   **closed stoma**

   b)   Circle the correct word(s) in each pair to complete the sentences below.

     i)   During the day water moves **into** / **out of** the guard cells by **osmosis** / **transpiration**,
making them **flaccid** / **turgid**. This **opens** / **closes** the stomata.

     ii)   During the night water moves **into** / **out of** the guard cells by **osmosis** / **transpiration**,
making them **flaccid** / **turgid**. This **opens** / **closes** the stomata.

Q4   Give three ways that transpiration **benefits** plants.

   1. ....

   2. ....

   3. ....

Water Flow Through Plants

Q5 Indicate whether each of the following statements is **true** or **false**.

True False

a) The transpiration rate decreases as the temperature increases. ☐ ☐

b) The more intense the light, the faster the transpiration rate. ☐ ☐

c) Transpiration happens more slowly when the air is humid. ☐ ☐

d) As the wind speed increases, the rate of transpiration decreases. ☐ ☐

Q6 Choose from the following words to complete the passage.

Each word can only be used once.

osmosis   leaves   evaporation   roots   flowers
phloem   diffusion   transpiration   xylem   stem

Most water leaves plants through the .... by the processes of

.... and .... This creates a slight shortage of

water in the .... which draws water from the rest of the plant

through the .... vessels. This causes more water to be drawn up

from the .... This whole process is called ....

Q7 Give three ways that plants in **hot climates** are adapted to **reduce** the amount of water lost.

1. ....

2. ....

3. ....

Q8 Stomata are different sizes at different **light intensities**.

a) Would you expect a plant's stomata to be open or closed on a bright sunny morning?
Explain your answer.

....

b) What happens to the stomata at night? What is the advantage of this?

....

c) If the supply of water to the roots of a plant dries up, the stomata close.
Give one **advantage** and one **disadvantage** of this mechanism for the plant.

....

....

Transport Systems in Plants

Q1 Put the following statements under the **correct heading** in the table.

- transport water
- made of living cells
- have end-plates
- have no end-plates
- transport food
- made of dead cells

Xylem vessels	Phloem vessels

Q2 The diagram shows a cross-section of a **leaf**.

a) Label a **xylem vessel**, and a **phloem vessel** on the diagram.

b) Circle a **vascular bundle** on the diagram.

Q3 The diagram shows a cross-section of a **plant's stem**.

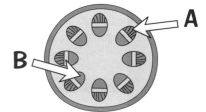

a) Name parts A and B.

A = ...

B = ...

b) Describe the function of **A** in the stem.

....

c) Describe one way that a cross-section of a root would look different from the cross-section of a stem.

....

Q4 Answer the following questions about **xylem**.

a) Name **two** substances transported by the xylem. ....

b) Describe the structure of a xylem tube.

....

....

c) Give another function of the xylem, other than transport. ....

d) How is the xylem adapted to carry out this function?

....

Minerals Needed for Healthy Growth

Q1 Draw lines to match the following **minerals** with their **functions** in plants.

MAGNESIUM		for making proteins
NITRATES		for making chlorophyll
PHOSPHATES		for making DNA and cell membranes
POTASSIUM		for helping enzymes to function

Q2 Spring has arrived but Pat has noticed that his **grain crop** is **not** growing well and the plants are stunted. He has grown grain in the same field for the last **three years**.

a) Suggest a reason why the grain crop is not growing properly.

....

b) Pat has been offered some **manure** for his field. The table shows the mineral content of different manures.

Which type of manure would you recommend Pat use? Explain your answer.

....

....

Material	% Nitrogen	% Phosphorus	% Potassium
Bullock manure	0.6	0.1	0.7
Cow manure	0.4	0.1	0.4
Horse manure	0.6	0.1	0.5
Pig manure	0.4	0.1	0.5
Poultry manure	1	0.4	0.6
Sheep manure	0.8	0.1	0.7

Q3 An investigation into the **mineral requirements** of plants was carried out as shown below.

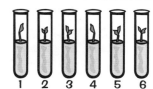

tubes 1 and 2:	complete mineral supply
tubes 3 and 4:	deficient in nitrates
tubes 5 and 6:	deficient in magnesium

a) Suggest why tubes 1 and 2 were included.

....

b) Predict how the seedlings in the following tubes will grow:

i) 3 and 4 ....

ii) 5 and 6 ....

c) Suggest why a sufficient amount of all the minerals except one was supplied to tubes 3, 4, 5 and 6.

....

....

94

Minerals Needed for Healthy Growth

Q4 A diagram of a **specialised plant cell** is shown.

a) Name the type of cell shown.

....

b) What is the main **function** of this type of cell?

....

c) How is this type of cell adapted for its function?

....

d) Explain why minerals are **not** absorbed from the soil by **diffusion**.

....

e) Explain how these specialised cells absorb mineral ions from the soil.
Use the words **active transport**, **concentration**, **respiration** and **energy** in your answer.

....

....

Q5 The levels of **magnesium** in fruit and vegetables tested in 1930 and 1980 are shown opposite.

a) Calculate the change in % magnesium content for each type of plant. Write your answers in the table. *Change in level = Final level minus initial level*

Plant	Magnesium content (%)		Change (%)
	1930	1980	
Brussel sprouts	19	8	
Carrots	12	3	
Onions	7.4	4	
Peas	30.2	34	
Potatoes	24.2	17	
Tomatoes	11	7	
Bananas	41.9	34	
Apples	4.7	3	
Strawberries	11.7	10	

b) State the general trend shown in the magnesium content.

....

....

c) How could you identify plants **deficient** in magnesium?

....

Top Tip: Whatever you do, **don't** say in an exam that minerals enter the root by diffusion. That would be **impossible**, because there are lower concentrations of mineral ions in the soil than in the root. **Active transport** uses energy to drag those mineral ions kicking and screaming in the wrong direction.

Module B4 — It's a Green World

Pyramids of Number and Biomass

Q1   A **pyramid of numbers** is shown below. Label the parts of the diagram using the following terms:

top consumer   primary consumer   producer   secondary consumer

a)

b)

c)

d)

Q2   **Tick** the correct columns to show which of the following are features of pyramids of **numbers** and which are features of pyramids of **biomass**. For each feature, you might need to tick **one** column, **both**, or **neither**.

Feature	Pyramid of numbers	Pyramid of biomass
Mass of organisms represented at each level.		
Always a pyramid shape.		
Each bar represents a step in a food chain.		
Always starts with a producer.		
Can only have 3 steps.		
Numbers are represented at each step.		

Pyramid of Tutankhamun

Pyramid of biomass

Q3   Complete the passage below by circling the most appropriate words.

As you move up trophic levels, the organisms are usually greater / fewer in number, the amount

of biomass increases / decreases, and there is a rise / fall in the amount of energy available.

Q4   A single **robin** has a mass of 15 g and eats caterpillars. Each robin eats 25 **caterpillars** that each have a mass of 2 g. The caterpillars feed on a total of 10 **stinging nettles** that together have a mass of 500 g. Study the pyramid diagrams shown and then answer the questions that follow.

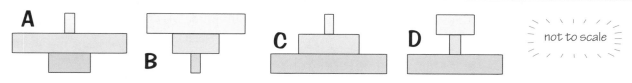

A   B   C   D   not to scale

a)   Which diagram is most likely to represent a pyramid of numbers for these organisms?   ....

b)   Which is most likely to represent a pyramid of biomass for these organisms?   ....

c)   Explain how you decided on your answer to part **b)** above.

....

d)   Where does the energy represented in the pyramid of biomass initially come from?

....

Energy Transfer and Energy Flow

Q1　Complete the sentences below by circling the correct words.

a)　Nearly all life on Earth depends on **food / energy** from the Sun.

b)　**Plants / Animals** can make their own food by a process called **photosynthesis / respiration**.

c)　To obtain energy animals must **decay / eat** plant material or other animals.

d)　Animals and plants release energy through the process of **photosynthesis / respiration**.

e)　Some of the energy released in animals is **gained / lost** through **growth / movement** (and in many other ways) before it reaches organisms at later steps of the food chain.

Q2　A **food chain** is shown in the diagram.

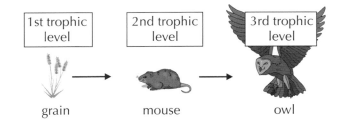

1st trophic level　　2nd trophic level　　3rd trophic level

grain　　　mouse　　　owl

a)　Put the following amounts of energy under the correct organisms.

500 kJ,　50 000 kJ,　8000 kJ

b)　Calculate the amount of energy lost between the:

i)　1st and 2nd trophic levels. ....

ii)　2nd and 3rd trophic levels. ....

c)　Calculate the efficiency of energy transfer from the:

i)　1st to 2nd trophic level. ....

ii)　2nd to 3rd trophic level. ....

Q3　Study the diagram of **energy transfer** shown.

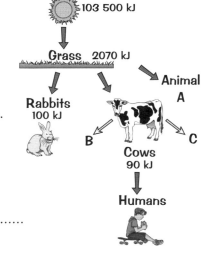

Sun 103 500 kJ

Grass 2070 kJ

Rabbits 100 kJ

Animal A

Cows 90 kJ

B　C

Humans

a)　Using the figures shown on the diagram, work out the percentage of the Sun's energy that is available in the grass.

....

b)　The efficiency of energy transfer from the grass to the next trophic level is 10%. Work out how much energy is available in animal A.

....

c)　**B** and **C** are processes that represent energy loss. Suggest what these processes might be.

....　　..

d)　Why do food chains rarely have more than five trophic levels?

....

....

Energy Transfer and Energy Flow

Q4   Another **food chain** is shown below.

leaf it out

	lettuce	Caterpillar	small bird	large bird
1	10 kJ	100 kJ	5000 kJ	30 000 kJ
2	30 000 kJ	30 000 kJ	30 000 kJ	30 000 kJ
3	30 000 kJ	5000 kJ	100 kJ	10 kJ

a)   Which row, 1, 2 or 3, shows the amount of energy available at each trophic level? ....

b)   Circle the answer below that shows how much energy is available to the caterpillar.

   5000 kJ   25 000 kJ   30 000 kJ

c)   Circle the answer below that shows how much energy is lost from the caterpillar to the small bird.

   100 kJ   4900 kJ   5000 kJ

Q5   An **aquatic food chain** is shown.

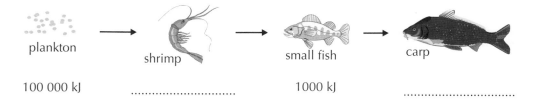

plankton   shrimp   small fish   carp

100 000 kJ   ....   1000 kJ   ....

a)   90 000 kJ is lost between the 1st trophic level (plankton) and the 2nd trophic level (shrimp).

   i)   On the diagram, write the amount of energy available in the shrimp for the small fish.

   ii)   Calculate the **efficiency** of energy transfer from the 1st to the 2nd trophic level.

   ....

b)   The energy transfer from the small fish to the carp is **5%** efficient.

   i)   On the diagram, write the amount of **energy** available in the **carp**.

   ii)   How much energy is **lost** from the food chain at this stage?

   ....

Biomass and Intensive Farming

Q1 Crops and meat from domestic animals are the most important food sources for many people.

a) Explain why meat production is not always the most **efficient** way of providing food.

....

b) Give two arguments **for** the inclusion of meat in the diet.

....

....

Q2 a) Explain why burning specifically planted fast-growing trees need **not** contribute to global warming.

....

....

b) What piece of equipment is biogas commercially made in?

....

c) Give one use of biogas.

....

Q3 Match up each **intensive farming** method below with the correct description and advantage.

using herbicides	kills insects	less energy wasted on movement and keeping warm
using insecticides	animals kept in small pens	more energy from the Sun is used by the crops
battery farming	kills weeds	less energy is transferred to another food chain

Q4 Give three **advantages** of using **biofuels** rather than fossil fuels.

1. ....

2. ....

3. ....

Q5 Many people feel that **battery farming** animals is **unethical**.

a) Give one advantage of battery farming.

....

b) Give one argument against battery farming.

....

Pesticides and Biological Control

Q1 a) What are pesticides and why are they used?

....

....

b) Give one problem that can be caused by the use of pesticides.

....

Q2 **Biological control** is an alternative to using pesticides.

a) What is biological control?

....

b) Give two examples of biological control.

1. ....

2. ....

c) Give an **advantage** and a **disadvantage** of using biological control.

Advantage: ....

Disadvantage: ....

Q3 The population of a species of bird of prey was **declining** as the shells of the eggs they were producing were too thin. **Pesticides** that were being sprayed onto fields near to the birds' habitat were found in the bodies of the birds at **toxic** levels.

Birds of prey only eat other animals and fish.

a) Explain how producing thin-shelled eggs due to the chemicals in the pesticides could lead to a decline in the bird population.

....

b) Suggest how pesticide that was sprayed onto crops was found in the birds.

....

c) The amount of pesticide sprayed onto the field was carefully controlled to keep the concentration below the toxic level. Suggest why the birds contained such large amounts of the pesticide.

....

....

Top Tips: Using pesticides and herbicides is a bit of a balancing act — they can **increase** crop yield, but do have an impact on the **environment**. Biological control may be the answer but there are still **disadvantages**. Remember — removing any organism from a food web can have **drastic effects**.

Pesticides and Biological Control

Q4 The diagram below shows a **food web**.

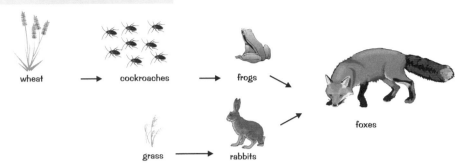

a) The cockroaches were sprayed with a pesticide to control the size of their population. Explain what effect this could have on the rest of the food web above.

....

....

....

b) Suggest how biological control could be used to reduce the cockroach population.

....

....

Q5 The table shows the size of the **pest population** and the **crop yield** in a farmer's field over five successive years.

Year	Estimated average pest population	Average crop yield (tonnes)
1	10 000	58
2	9000	66
3	9800	60
4	2000	88
5	2200	86

a) Explain the relationship between the size of the pest population and the crop yield.

....

....

b) In which year do you think the use of a pesticide was introduced? ....

c) Pesticides are expensive. Do you think this farmer's use of pesticides is likely to be cost-effective? Explain your answer.

....

....

Alternatives to Intensive Farming

Q1 Plants can be grown without soil.

a) What is the name of this technique?

....

b) What are the plants grown in?

....

c) Give an example of a plant that is often grown in this way.

....

d) Some of the things that need to be considered for this technique are listed below.
Tick to show whether each is an **advantage** or **disadvantage**.

Feature	Advantage	Disadvantage
i) Amount of land required.	☐	☐
ii) The set-up cost.	☐	☐
iii) Amount of weeding required.	☐	☐
iv) Can be used to grow plants in places with poor soil.	☐	☐
v) Support is needed by the plants.	☐	☐
vi) Special soluble nutrients are needed.	☐	☐

Farmer Giles' methods were intense

Q2 For each of the **intensive farming methods** below suggest an **organic farming alternative** and give one **advantage** of the alternative method.

a) **Using insecticides:** alternative method — ....

Advantage: ....

b) **Using herbicides:** alternative method — ....

Advantage: ....

c) **Using chemical fertilisers:** alternative method — ....

Advantage: ....

Top Tips: A large proportion of the food on supermarket shelves is produced by **intensive farming**, but **organic products** have increased in popularity recently. You'll need to know what the alternative, organic methods involve and all their **advantages** and **disadvantages**.

Alternatives to Intensive Farming

Q3 A farmer is considering using **manure and compost** instead of chemical fertilisers, and **weeding** instead of herbicides. Comment on the implications for the farmer in terms of **cost**, the amount of **labour** needed and the effect on the **environment**.

a) Cost ....

....

....

b) Amount of labour ....

....

....

c) Effect on the environment ....

....

....

Q4 The table below shows the **energy** for activities like ploughing and weeding that two farmers put into their farms over a year. The table also shows the amount of food energy **produced** by the farms. One farm is an **intensive** farm and one farm is an **organic** farm, and they both produce cereal.

MJ = 1 million joules

	Energy input per hectare in MJ	Food energy produced per hectare in MJ
Intensive Farm	12 000	4 000
Organic Farm	3 500	1 900

a) Calculate how many MJ of food are produced for each MJ of energy put into each farm.

Intensive farm ....

Organic farm ....

b) Explain why the organic farm would need to be larger than the intensive one in order to produce the same amount of cereal.

....

....

c) Which of these two farms would you expect to employ more staff? Explain your answer.

....

....

Decay

Q1 Use the words provided to fill in the gaps in the paragraph below.

elements   decomposition   bacteria   dead   water   soil   warmth   carbon   nitrogen   waste

Micro-organisms such as .... and fungi in the ....

and air break down .... organisms and .... — this is

called .... This recycles .... such as

.... and .... The micro-organisms require oxygen,

.... and .... to break down organic material.

Q2 The **rate** of decay depends on three main things — **temperature**, **moisture** and **oxygen**.

a) Sketch a line on the graph provided to show what you think will happen to
the rate of decay as **temperature increases**. (Assume the temperature doesn't
rise enough to damage the microbes and there is plenty of water and oxygen.)

b) Explain the shape of the graph you have drawn.

....

....

c) If you were to carry out an investigation to test your prediction,
name **two** variables you would need to keep constant.

....

....

graph: rate of decay (y-axis) vs temperature (x-axis)

d) A list of **three** sets of conditions is shown in the box.
Rank the sets of conditions from 1 to 3, 1 being the best
for decay and 3 being the worst for decay.

Conditions	Rank
Dry, cold, no oxygen	....
Moist, warm, oxygen	....
Moist, cold, no oxygen	....

Q3 Draw lines to link the **food preservation methods** with how they reduce decay.

Canning	lowers the pH, which inhibits the enzymes of the micro-organisms
Freezing	without water, micro-organisms die
Pickling	microbes can't respire and reproduce at low temperatures
Drying	stops food being exposed to microbes

Q4 Explain how storing tuna in **brine** helps to preserve it.

....

Top Tips: This is easy as long as you know about the conditions microbes like for decay —
warm, **damp** and with **oxygen available**. Then it's simple to remember the methods we use to **stop** them.

The Carbon Cycle

Q1 Decaying material is broken down by two types of organism — **saprophytes** and **detritivores**.

a) Complete the following passage using the words provided.

speeding up   larger   detritivores   slowing down   detritus   smaller   saprophytes

Earthworms, maggots and woodlice are all examples of ...., which

feed on dead and decaying material (or ....). They break the

decaying material into .... bits. This gives a ....

surface area for decomposers to work on, ... decay.

b) Explain how saprophytes feed using enzymes.

....

....

....

Q2 Follow the instructions below to complete the diagram of part of the **carbon cycle**.

$$CO_2 \text{ in the air}$$

| plant | | animal |

a) Add an arrow or arrows labelled **P** to represent **photosynthesis**.

b) Add an arrow or arrows labelled **R** to represent **respiration**.

c) Add an arrow or arrows labelled **F** to represent **feeding**.

100% pure carbon

Q3 **Living things** and the **air** are both involved in the carbon cycle.

a) Number the sentences below to show how carbon moves from the air to living things.

☐ Animals eat the plants' carbon compounds.

☐ Carbon is contained in the air as carbon dioxide.

☐ Plants and animals die.

☐ Plants take in carbon dioxide for photosynthesis and make carbon compounds.

b) Add a fifth point to complete the cycle and explain how carbon in dead organisms is returned to the air.

Point 5: ....

Module B4 — It's a Green World

The Carbon Cycle

Q4   **Carbon** is a very important element that is constantly being recycled.

a)   What is the one way that carbon is removed from the atmosphere?

....

b)   In what form is carbon removed from the atmosphere?

....

c)   What is this carbon converted into by plants?

....

d)   How is this carbon passed on through the food chain?

....

e)   By what process do **all** living organisms return carbon to the air?

....

Q5   The diagram below shows a version of the **carbon cycle**.

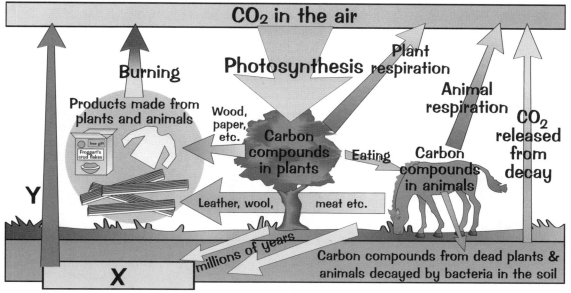

a)   Name substance **X** shown on the diagram above. ....

b)   Explain why substance **X** contains carbon.

....

....

c)   Name the process labelled **Y** on the diagram above. ....

The Nitrogen Cycle

Q1 Circle the correct word(s) to complete each sentence below.

a) Nitrogen is needed to make **protein** / **carbohydrate** / **fat**.

b) **Air** is **100%** / **21%** / **78%** nitrogen.

c) The nitrogen found in air is **a reactive gas** / **an unreactive gas** / **an unreactive liquid**.

Q2 Match up each type of **organism** below with the way it obtains **nitrogen**.

Plants	By breaking down dead organisms and animal waste
Animals	By absorbing nitrates from the soil
Bacteria	By eating other organisms

Q3 The nitrogen cycle is dependent on a number of different types of **micro-organism**. Explain the role of each of the following types of **bacteria** in the nitrogen cycle.

Type of bacteria — **Role in the nitrogen cycle**

a) Decomposers ....

b) Nitrifying bacteria ....

c) Denitrifying bacteria ....

d) Nitrogen-fixing bacteria ....

Q4 Below is a diagram of the **nitrogen cycle**. Explain what is shown in the stages labelled:

a) X ....

b) Y ....

c) Z ....

Q5 A farmer was told that if he planted **legume plants** his soil would become more **fertile**. Explain how the legume plants would increase the fertility of his soil.

....

....

Mixed Questions — Module B4

Q1 The diagram below shows a **food chain** observed on the savannahs of Tanzania. It also shows the amount of **energy** available in each trophic level.

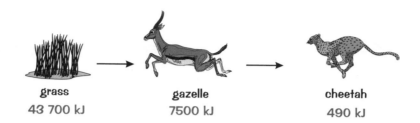

grass
43 700 kJ

gazelle
7500 kJ

cheetah
490 kJ

a) **i)** How much energy is lost from the 1st trophic level (grass) to the next (gazelle)?

....

ii) Calculate the efficiency of this energy transfer.

....

b) Suggest two ways in which energy might be lost by the gazelle.

....

....

c) **Carbon** also moves through the food chain. It is continuously being **recycled** from one form to another as the diagram below shows.

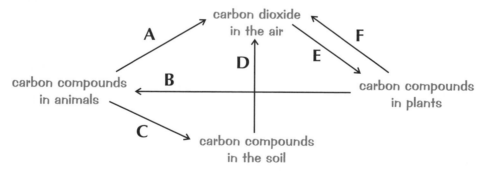

Name the processes labelled **A**, **B**, **C**, **D**, **E** and **F** in the diagram.

A .... B ....

C .... D ....

E .... F ....

d) Cheetahs don't always eat all of the meat on a gazelle. What is not eaten begins to **decompose**. The savannahs are warm and open (giving a good supply of air) but quite dry. Explain how these conditions will influence the rate at which the meat decomposes.

....

....

Mixed Questions — Module B4

Q2 Diagrams **A**, **B**, **C**, **D** and **E** show some **pyramids of number** and **pyramids of biomass** based on data collected from Farmer MacDonald's land.

A   B   C   D   E

a) Which of the pyramids could be pyramids of number? ....

b) Which of the pyramids could be pyramids of biomass? Explain your answer.

....

....

c) Which of the pyramids could be a pyramid of number to represent the following food chains?

i) Oak tree → caterpillars → blackbirds → buzzards ....

ii) Oak leaves → snails → hedgehogs → fleas ....

d) Farmer MacDonald uses **chemical pesticides** on his crops.

i) Explain why he uses these chemicals.

....

....

ii) What effect might the use of these pesticides have on the **buzzards** in the food chain in c) i)?

....

....

e) Suggest two ways that organic farming can help to conserve endangered species.

....

....

f) Farmer MacDonald also puts **fertiliser** on his crops. The fertiliser he uses provides the crops with essential minerals to ensure healthy growth.

i) Which two minerals are most important for photosynthesis?

....

ii) Which mineral is vital for making proteins? ....

iii) How can use of fertilisers damage the environment?

....

....

Mixed Questions — Module B4

Q3   **Legumes** are plants that have nodules on their roots containing **nitrogen-fixing bacteria**.

a)   Suggest why some farmers rotate their crops, alternating between cereals and legumes in a field.

....

b)   Explain how and why an insufficient nitrogen intake affects a plant's development.

....

....

c)   Another reason some farmers rotate crops is to prevent the build-up of harmful pathogens.
Mould is a fungus and a significant **plant pest**. This diagram shows mould growing on a **leaf**.

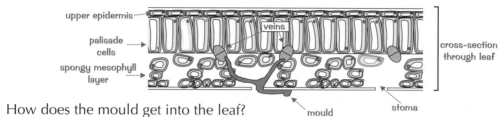

i)   How does the mould get into the leaf?

....

ii)   Which type of vessel in the leaf is the mould invading in the diagram?
Suggest why the mould invades this type of vessel.

....

....

Q4   A student carried out a series of experiments into **water movement**.

a)   In the first experiment potato chips were placed in different solutions. Their mass was recorded at
the start and again after one day. The results are shown in the following table.

tube	start mass, g	end mass, g
A	1.20	1.45
B	1.40	1.21
C	1.32	1.32

Which tube (A, B or C) contained:

i)   pure water? ....

ii)   dilute sugar solution? ....

iii)   concentrated sugar solution? ....

b)   In the second experiment **water** loss from a leafy shoot was measured. The shoot was exposed
to **different conditions** and the water loss measured each time. The results are shown on the
graph. Complete the table to show which line represents each set of conditions.

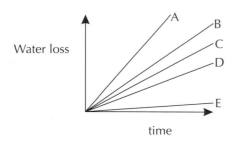

Treatment	Line
kept in normal conditions	C
covered, clear plastic bag	
fanned, cool air	
fanned, warm air	
covered, black plastic bag	

Acids and Bases

Q1   Define the following terms.

a)   Acid ....

b)   Base ....

c)   Alkali ....

Q2 a)   Which is the correct word equation for a **neutralisation reaction**? Circle your answer.

salt + acid → base + water   acid + base → salt + water

acid + water → base + salt

b)   Which of the ions, $\boxed{\textbf{H}^+ \textbf{ or OH}^-}$, is found in the largest quantity in:

i)   acidic solutions?   ....

ii)   alkaline solutions?   ....

iii)   a solution with a pH of 10?   ....

iv)   lemon juice?   ....

Q3   **Indigestion** is caused by too much acid in the stomach.
Antacid tablets contain bases which neutralise the excess acid.

Joey wanted to test whether some antacid tablets really did **neutralise acid**. He added a tablet to some hydrochloric acid, stirred it until it dissolved and tested the pH of the solution. Further tests were carried out after dissolving a second, third and fourth tablet.
His results are shown in the table.

Number of Tablets	pH
0	1
1	2
2	3
3	7
4	9

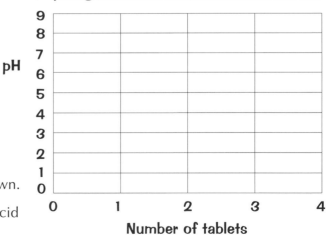

pH against no. of tablets added to acid

a)   i)   Plot a graph of the results on the grid shown.

ii)   Describe how the pH changes when antacid tablets are added to the acid.

....

iii)   How many tablets were needed to neutralise the acid? ....

b)   Joey tested another brand of tablets and found that **two** tablets neutralised the same volume of acid. On the graph, sketch the results you might expect for these tablets.

Acids and Bases

Q4 Complete the following sentences with a single word.

a) Solutions which are not acidic or alkaline are said to be ....

b) Universal indicator is a combination of different coloured ....

c) When a substance is neutral it has a pH of ....

Q5 Ants' stings hurt because of the **formic acid** they release. The pH measurements of some household substances are given in the table.

SUBSTANCE	pH
lemon juice	4
baking soda	9
caustic soda	14
soap powder	11

a) Describe how you could test the formic acid to find its pH value.

....

b) Suggest a substance from the list that could be used to relieve the discomfort of an ant sting. Explain your answer.

....

....

c) Explain why **universal indicator** only gives an **estimate** of the pH of a substance.

....

Q6 Modern industry uses thousands of tonnes of **sulfuric acid** per day.

a) The pie chart shows the major uses of the sulfuric acid produced by a particular plant. What is the **main use** of the sulfuric acid from this plant?

....

Fibres 9%
Detergents 11%
Paints and Pigments 15%
Other Chemicals 16%
Fertilisers 32%
Other Uses 17%

b) Give two uses of sulfuric acid in the car manufacturing industry.

1. .... 2. ....

c) Which of the following compounds found in fertilisers is manufactured from sulfuric acid?

ammonium nitrate   ammonium sulfate   ammonium phosphate   potassium nitrate

d) Describe how sulfuric acid is used in the preparation of metal surfaces.

....

....

Top Tips: Ahh... acids and bases. They pop up everywhere. And I mean EVERYWHERE. The chemistry lab, the human body, vehicles, poisons and antidotes, even in the kitchen sink.

Reactions of Acids

Q1   Fill in the blanks to complete the word equations for
acids reacting with **metal oxides** and **metal hydroxides**.

a)   hydrochloric acid + lead oxide → .... chloride + water

b)   nitric acid + copper hydroxide → copper .... + water

c)   sulfuric acid + zinc oxide → zinc sulfate + ...

d)   hydrochloric acid + ... oxide → nickel .... + ...

e)   .... acid + copper oxide → .... nitrate + ...

f)   sulfuric acid + ... hydroxide → sodium .... + ...

Q2 a)   Put a tick in the box next to any of the sentences below that are **true**.

  i)   Alkalis are bases which can't dissolve in water.   ☐

  ii)   Acids react with metal oxides to form a salt and water.   ☐

  iii)   Hydrogen gas is formed when an acid reacts with an alkali.   ☐

  iv)   Salts and water are formed when acids react with metal hydroxides.   ☐

  v)   Calcium hydroxide is an acid that dissolves in water.   ☐

b)   Use the formulas below to write **symbol equations** for two acid / base reactions.

H_2SO_4 H_2O CuO H_2O $NaCl$ HCl $CuSO_4$ $NaOH$

  1. ....

  2. ....

Q3   **Ammonia** can be neutralised by **nitric acid** to form **ammonium nitrate**.

a)   Circle the correct formula for ammonia below.

  NH_4NO_3 NH_4Cl NH_3 NH_2 NH_4

b)   Write down the symbol equation for the reaction between ammonia and nitric acid.

  ....

c)   How is this neutralisation reaction different from most neutralisation reactions?

  ....

d)   Why is ammonium nitrate a particularly good fertiliser?

  ....

Reactions of Acids

Q4 a) Complete the following equations.

i) H_2SO_4 + ... → $CuSO_4$ + H_2O

ii) $2HNO_3$ + MgO → $Mg(NO_3)_2$ + ...

iii) .... + KOH → KCl + H_2O

iv) $2HCl$ + ... → $ZnCl_2$ + H_2O

v) H_2SO_4 + $2NaOH$ → .... + ...

b) **Balance** the following acid/base reactions.

i) $NaOH$ + H_2SO_4 → Na_2SO_4 + H_2O

ii) $Mg(OH)_2$ + HNO_3 → $Mg(NO_3)_2$ + H_2O

iii) NH_3 + H_3PO_4 → $(NH_4)_3PO_4$

Q5 **Acids** react with **metal carbonates** in neutralisation reactions.

a) Complete the following word equations.

i) hydrochloric acid + ... carbonate →

copper .... + water + ...

ii) .... acid + magnesium .... →

.... nitrate + ... + carbon dioxide

iii) sulfuric acid + lithium carbonate → .... + ...+ ....

b) Complete and balance the following symbol equations.

i) .... HCl + $CaCO_3$ → $CaCl_2$ + ... + CO_2

ii) H_2SO_4 + ... → Na_2SO_4 + ... + ...

iii) .... + ... → $Ca(NO_3)_2$ + H_2O + CO_2

iv) .... + Na_2CO_3 → .... $NaCl$ + ... + ...

c) Keith wants to confirm that the gas released when he reacts calcium carbonate with hydrochloric acid is **carbon dioxide**. Outline an **experimental procedure** he could use to test the gas.

....

....

Relative Formula Mass

Q1   What are the **relative atomic masses** (A_r) of the following:

a) Magnesium ....

b) Neon ....

c) Oxygen ....

d) Hydrogen ....

e) C ....

f) Cu ....

g) K ....

h) Ca ....

i) Cl ....

Q2   Identify the elements A, B and C.

> Element A has an A_r of 4.
> Element B has an A_r 3 times that of element A.
> Element C has an A_r 4 times that of element A.

Element A = ...

Element B = ...

Element C = ...

Q3 a)   Explain how the **relative formula mass** of a **compound** is calculated.

....

b)   What are the **relative formula masses** (M_r) of the following:

i)   Water, H_2O ....

ii)   Potassium hydroxide, KOH ....

iii)   Nitric acid, HNO_3 ....

iv)   Ammonium nitrate, NH_4NO_3 ....

v)   Calcium nitrate, $Ca(NO_3)_2$ ....

vi)   Iron(III) hydroxide, $Fe(OH)_3$ ....

Q4   The equation below shows a reaction between element X and water.
The sum of the M_r of the **reactants** is **114**. What is element X?

$$2X + 2H_2O \rightarrow 2XOH + H_2$$

....

....

Calculating Masses in Reactions

Q1 Anna burns **10 g** of **magnesium** in air to produce **magnesium oxide** (MgO).

a) Write out the **balanced equation** for this reaction.

....

b) Calculate the mass of **magnesium oxide** that's produced.

....

....

....

Q2 What mass of **sodium** is needed to make **2 g** of **sodium oxide**? $4Na + O_2 \rightarrow 2Na_2O$

....

....

....

Q3 **Aluminium** and **iron oxide** (Fe_2O_3) react together to produce **aluminium oxide** (Al_2O_3) and **iron**.

a) Write out the **balanced equation** for this reaction.

....

b) What **mass** of iron is produced from **20 g** of iron oxide?

....

....

....

Q4 When heated, **limestone** ($CaCO_3$) decomposes to form **calcium oxide** (CaO) and **carbon dioxide**.

How many **kilograms** of limestone are needed to make **100 kilograms** of **calcium oxide**?

The calculation is exactly the same — just use 'kg' instead of 'g'. ....

....

....

Calculating Masses in Reactions

Q5 **Iron oxide** is reduced to **iron** inside a blast furnace using carbon. There are **three** stages involved.

Stage A	$C + O_2 \rightarrow CO_2$
Stage B	$CO_2 + C \rightarrow 2CO$
Stage C	$3CO + Fe_2O_3 \rightarrow 2Fe + 3CO_2$

a) If **10 g** of **carbon** are used in stage B, and all the carbon monoxide produced gets used in stage C, what **mass** of CO_2 is produced in **stage C**?

....

....

....

....

Work out the mass of CO at the end of stage B first.

b) Suggest how the CO_2 might be used after stage C.

....

Look at where CO_2 is used.

Q6 **Sodium sulfate** (Na_2SO_4) is made by reacting **sodium hydroxide** (NaOH) with **sulfuric acid** (H_2SO_4). **Water** is also produced.

a) Write out the **balanced equation** for this reaction.

....

b) What mass of **sodium hydroxide** is needed to make **75 g** of **sodium sulfate**?

....

....

....

....

c) What mass of **water** is formed when **50 g** of **sulfuric acid** reacts?

....

....

....

....

Percentage Yield

Q1   James wanted to produce **silver chloride** (AgCl). He added a carefully measured mass
of silver nitrate to an excess of dilute hydrochloric acid. An **insoluble white salt** formed.

   a)   Write down the formula for calculating the **percentage yield** of a reaction.

   b)   James calculated that he should get 2.7 g of silver chloride, but he only got 1.2 g.
What was the **percentage yield**?

   ....

   ....

Q2   Explain how the following factors can affect the **percentage yield**.

   a)   Heating ....

   ....

   b)   Filtration (when you want to keep the liquid) ....

   ....

   c)   Transferring liquids ....

   ....

   d)   Evaporation ....

   ....

Q3   Aaliya and Natasha mixed together barium chloride ($BaCl_2$) and sodium sulfate (Na_2SO_4) in
a beaker. An **insoluble** substance formed. They **filtered** the solution to obtain the solid
substance, and then transferred the solid to a clean piece of **filter paper** and left it to dry.

   a)   Aaliya calculated that they should produce a yield of **15 g** of barium sulfate.
However, after completing the experiment they found they had only obtained **6 g**.

   Calculate the **percentage yield** for this reaction.

   ....

   ....

   b)   Suggest two reasons why their actual yield was lower than their predicted yield.

   1. ....

   2. ....

Fertilisers

Q1   Choose from the words to fill in the blanks below.

non-essential	sodium	proteins	yield	growth
phosphorus	carbohydrates	previous	essential	

Fertilisers are used to increase crop .... They provide plants with

.... elements needed for ...., making crops grow

faster and bigger. These elements include nitrogen, ... and potassium.

Nitrogen is used in plants to make .... Fertilisers replace elements in

the soil that a .... crop could have used up.

Q2   Sophie is concerned about the amount of **fertiliser** that gets washed into **rivers**.

a)   Circle any of the following compounds that can be used as fertilisers.

ammonium nitrate   urea   potassium nitrate   nitric acid   copper carbonate   oxygen   ammonium phosphate

b)   Sophie suggests trapping the fertiliser compounds in **insoluble** pellets. Why is this idea flawed?

....

Q3   Tamsin prepares **ammonium sulfate** in the lab using the apparatus shown in the diagram. She finds that she needs 12.6 cm³ of sulfuric acid to **just** change the colour of the methyl orange indicator from yellow to red.

a)   Suggest what piece of apparatus Tamsin used to accurately measure 25.0 cm³ of ammonia solution.

....

b)   Name the apparatus shown in the diagram that's used to add the sulfuric acid into the ammonia solution.

....

c)   What type of reaction is occurring? ....

Tamsin repeats the experiment to obtain **pure** crystals of ammonium sulfate.

d)   What important **difference** must she make to her experimental procedure to produce **pure** ammonium sulfate?

....

e)   What volume of sulfuric acid must she add? ....

f)   How can Tamsin get ammonium sulfate crystals from her ammonium sulfate solution?

....

....

Fertilisers

Q4   Number the following stages 1– 6 to describe the process of **eutrophication**.

☐   There is a rapid growth of algae, called an 'algal bloom'.

☐   Plants die because they don't receive enough light.

☐   The amounts of nitrates and phosphates in the water increase.

☐   Fish and other living organisms start to die.

☐   Excess fertiliser runs off fields into rivers and streams.

☐   Decomposers feed off the dead plants, using up all the oxygen in the water.

Q5   Calculate the **relative formula masses**, M_r, of the following fertilisers.

a)   potassium nitrate, KNO_3 ....

b)   ammonium sulfate, $(NH_4)_2SO_4$ ....

c)   ammonium phosphate, $(NH_4)_3PO_4$ ....

Q6   Calculate the **percentage mass** of nitrogen in the following compounds.

Use the equation
$$\% \text{ mass} = \frac{(A_r \times n)}{M_r} \times 100$$

a)   ammonium nitrate, NH_4NO_3

....

b)   urea, $CO(NH_2)_2$

....

Q7   Farmer Freda wants to give a field of crops exactly **50 kg** of potassium.

Start by calculating the % mass of potassium in potassium nitrate.

a)   What mass of potassium nitrate fertiliser, KNO_3, should she apply?

....

....

b)   In applying the potassium nitrate in **a)**, what mass of **nitrogen** will also have been provided?

....

....

Q8   Suggest **three** pieces of advice on the use of fertilisers that could be given to farmers to help prevent **eutrophication**.

1. ....

2. ....

3. ....

The Haber Process

Q1 The Haber process is used to make **ammonia**.

a) The equation for the reaction is

$$N_2 + 3H_2 \rightleftharpoons 2NH_3$$

i) Name the reactants in the forward reaction ....

ii) Which side of the equation has more molecules? ....

b) Give a **use** of ammonia.

....

Q2 The **industrial conditions** for the Haber process are carefully chosen.

a) What conditions are used? Tick one box.

☐ 1000 atmospheres, 450 °C	☐ 200 atmospheres, 1000 °C	☐ 450 atmospheres, 200 °C	☐ 200 atmospheres, 450 °C

b) Give two reasons why the pressure used is chosen.

1. ....

2. ....

Q3 In the Haber process, the forward reaction is **exothermic**.

a) What effect will raising the temperature have on the **amount** of ammonia formed?

....

b) Explain why a high temperature is used industrially.

....

c) What happens to the leftover nitrogen and hydrogen? ....

Q4 The Haber process uses an **iron catalyst**.

a) What effect does this have on the % yield? ....

b) Iron catalysts are cheap. What effect does using one have on the **cost** of producing the ammonia? Explain your answer.

....

....

Top Tips: Changing the conditions in a reversible reaction to get more product sounds great, but don't forget that these conditions might be too difficult or expensive for factories to produce, or they might make the reaction too slow to be profitable.

Module C4 — Chemical Economics

Minimising the Cost of Production

Q1 Use the following words to complete the blanks.

yield	sufficient	optimum	rate	recycled	lowest

.... conditions are chosen to give the .... production cost per kg of product. This may mean that the conditions used do not have the highest .... of reaction or the highest percentage .... of product. However, both the rate and the yield must be high enough to give a .... daily yield of product. A low percentage yield is acceptable if the starting materials can be .... and reacted again.

Q2 Explain how the following affect the **production costs** of making a new substance.

a) Catalysts ....

....

b) Recycling raw materials ....

....

c) Automation ....

....

d) High temperatures ....

....

Q3 A pharmaceutical company tests two production processes for producing a new drug. Rupert records both the total **production cost** and the total **yield** for each process over a one-week period.

a) Calculate the cost per g of drug for each process.

....

....

....

....

....

b) Suggest why the company decides to use process B, even though it has a higher production cost.

....

Detergents and Dry-Cleaning

Q1 Match the following terms to their correct descriptions.

solvent   A substance that's dissolved in a liquid.

solution   A liquid mixture made from dissolving a substance in a liquid.

solute   A liquid that can dissolve a substance.

Q2 Some fabrics need to be **dry-cleaned**.

a) What is dry-cleaning? ....

b) Name **one** solvent commonly used in dry-cleaning. ....

c) Give two reasons why it is necessary to dry-clean some clothes rather than using a detergent.

1. ....

2. ....

Q3 The diagram shows a detergent molecule.

a) Complete the diagram by labelling the **hydrophilic** and **hydrophobic** sections of the molecule.

....

b) Which section of the molecule is attracted to:

i) water molecules? ....

ii) grease and oil? ....

c) The first detergents used by humans thousands of years ago were soaps made from fats.

i) What disadvantage do soaps have when used in **hard water** areas? ....

ii) What raw material are modern synthetic detergents made from? ....

Q4 Fill in blanks using the appropriate words below.

| water | stain | intermolecular | disperse |
| intramolecular | pull | grease | sugar | react |

Detergents work by helping dirt to .... in water. Normally oil or

.... stains do not mix with water. The hydrophobic tail attaches

to the fat molecules in the stain with .... forces. The hydrophilic

head is surrounded by .... molecules outside the stain.

The movement of the washing machine helps the detergent molecules to

.... away droplets of oil into the water, leaving the fabric clean.

Detergents and Dry-Cleaning

Q5 Many modern detergents used for washing clothes are 'biological'.

a) What is the difference between biological and non-biological detergents?

....

b) Why do biological detergents become less effective at temperatures above 40 °C?

....

c) Circle the types of stain below that biological detergents should be particularly effective at cleaning.

paint   blood   grass   tomato ketchup   engine oil

Q6 Felicity works for a chemical company that is developing a new washing powder. She tests five different powders and records their cleaning effectiveness at different temperatures and against a range of different stains. She uses a scale of 1 (poor) to 10 (excellent).

a) Which powder is best at cleaning grass stains at 40 °C?

....

		Washing powder				
		A	B	C	D	E
Effectiveness	at 40 °C	9	3	5	7	7
	at 60 °C	3	3	9	8	4
	Against tomato stains (at 40 °C)	8	1	5	4	10
	Against grass stains (at 40 °C)	8	4	5	7	3

b) Which powders could be biological detergents? Give a reason for your answer.

....

....

....

Q7 Emily is trying to decide what temperature is best to wash her clothes at.

a) Why are **high** temperatures usually best for washing clothes?

....

b) Why shouldn't you wash clothes made from the following materials at high temperatures?

i) Wool ....

ii) Nylon ....

c) Emily's friend says, 'Washing clothes at high temperatures is environmentally unfriendly.' Explain why.

....

....

Detergents and Dry-Cleaning

Q8   Simon sets up a test to find which of four different washing powders is most effective.
He cuts a white cotton cloth into four pieces and stains each one with a different substance.

The diagram shows the four different washes that he has planned.

Describe why Simon's experiment is **not** a fair test.

....

....

....

Egg yolk
Powder A

Blackcurrant
Powder B

Curry
Powder C

Engine oil
Powder D

Q9   Use these words to complete the blanks.

| ionic | intramolecular | solute | solvent | detergents |
| intermolecular | surrounded | covalent | solution | bonds |

When a solid is dissolved in a liquid, ... forces occur between

the liquid molecules and the solid particles. These forces help to break

.... between the solid particles and the solid breaks up. A solid is

dissolved when its particles are completely .... by liquid molecules.

.... are used to help water dissolve substances. Some substances

will not dissolve in water at all and another .... is required.

Q10   A chemical company is testing three new solvents for dry-cleaning.

a)   What mass of solvent A is needed to dissolve 50 g of paint?

....

....

....

	Solvent		
	A	**B**	**C**
Cost per 100 g (£)	0.40	0.15	0.20
Solubility of paint (g per 100 g of solvent)	12.1	0.1	10.3

b)   Which solvent would you expect to form the strongest intermolecular forces with paint molecules?
Explain your answer.

....

c)   Which solvent would you choose to buy if you were a buyer for a dry-cleaning company?
Explain your choice.

....

....

Module C4 — Chemical Economics

Chemical Production

Q1 Suggest whether **continuous** or **batch** production would be used to make the following chemicals.

a) Perfumes ....

b) Sulfuric acid ....

c) Ammonia ....

d) Paints ....

Q2 Widely used chemicals are often produced by **continuous production**.

a) Circle the correct words to complete the following sentences.

> Continuous production is often used for the small-scale / large-scale production of chemicals. It's highly automated / labour-intensive, which means that there are low / high labour costs. Continuous production means that products of a high / low consistency can be produced with a high / low risk of contamination.

b) State two **disadvantages** of continuous production.

1. ....

2. ....

Q3 **Batch production** is used to produce specialist chemicals.

a) Use these words to complete the blanks about batch production.

inflexible   high   small   contamination   large   versatile   low

> Batch production is often used for manufacturing .... quantities of specialist chemicals. The advantages of batch production are that the plant is .... (allowing for many different products to be made), and that the costs of plant equipment are .... Disadvantages of batch production include the .... labour costs and the increased risk of ....

b) Why are **pharmaceutical drugs** usually manufactured using batch production?

....

c) In the context of batch production, what is '**downtime**'?

....

....

Module C4 — Chemical Economics

Chemical Production

Q4 Compounds used in pharmaceutical drugs are often extracted from **plants**.

a) Describe the following steps in the extraction process.

A   B   C

Step A ....

Step B ....

Step C ....

b) New drugs may be tested on animals before being sold.

i) Give one argument for and one argument against testing new drugs on **animals**.

For ....

Against ....

ii) After animal testing, why are **human trials** of drugs also necessary?

....

Q5 Tony decides his pharmaceutical company should develop and manufacture a new drug.

a) Suggest one thing that Tony needs to research before developing a new drug.

....

b) Give two reasons why the **research** and **development** of new pharmaceutical drugs is expensive.

1. ....

2. ....

c) Give two reasons why the **manufacturing** process of pharmaceutical drugs is expensive.

1. ....

2. ....

d) Explain why it might be a long time before Tony gets back his initial investment.

....

....

....

Module C4 — Chemical Economics

Allotropes of Carbon

Q1   Diamond is an allotrope of carbon.

a)   Circle the correct words to complete the sentences below about diamond.

> Diamond has a **simple molecular / giant covalent** structure. Each carbon atom in diamond forms **three / four** bonds with neighbouring atoms. Diamond is **soft / hard** and has a **low / high** melting point, which makes it ideal for use in **lubricants / cutting tools**.

b)   Why is diamond **unable** to conduct electricity?

....

c)   Name two properties of diamond that make it useful for **jewellery**.

1. ....   2. ....

Q2   Graphite is another allotrope of carbon.

a)   Choose from these words to complete the blanks below.

| four | red | tools | lubricant | tightly | three | high |
| low | black | loosely | slide | delocalised |

> Graphite is made of layers of carbon that are held .... together.
> It is .... in colour. Within the layers, each carbon atom forms
> .... covalent bonds. These strong covalent bonds give graphite a
> .... melting point. Between the layers there is only a weak
> attraction. This enables the layers to .... easily over each other,
> which makes it useful as a ....

b)   Explain why graphite is **able** to conduct electricity.

....

....

c)   Give two reasons why graphite is used in pencil leads.

1. ....

2. ....

Top Tips: There's more than one allotrope of carbon you've got to know about and each one is well suited to its uses. You wouldn't use diamonds in your tennis racket after all. Well, unless you were exceptionally rich, and then you could have diamonds on the soles of your shoes as well.

Allotropes of Carbon

Q3 The diagram shows a molecule of **buckminsterfullerene**.

a) What is the **molecular formula** of buckminsterfullerene? ....

b) How many covalent bonds does each carbon atom form? ....

c) Can buckminsterfullerene conduct electricity? Explain your answer.

....

....

d) Fullerenes can be used to 'cage' other molecules. Give a potential use for this technology.

....

Q4 Nanoparticles are really tiny particles, between 1 and 100 nanometres across.

a) How many nanometres are there in **1 mm**? $1 \, m = 1 \times 10^9 \, nm$

....

....

b) Describe an example of a nanoparticle having very different properties to the 'bulk' chemical.

....

c) Explain how nanoparticles are useful in producing industrial **catalysts**.

....

....

Q5 Fullerenes can be joined together to make nanotubes.

Piccadilly

a) What are nanotubes?

....

b) Give **two** properties of nanotubes that make them useful in **electrical circuits**.

....

....

c) Give a property of nanotubes that makes them useful in **tennis rackets**.

....

Water Purity

Q1   There are limited water resources in the UK.

a)   Which one of the following water resources is a source of 'groundwater'? Circle your answer.

reservoirs   aquifers   rivers   lakes

b)   Name three important uses of water in **industrial processes**.

1. ....

2. ....

3. ....

Q2   Suggest **one** way that water could be **conserved** by:

a)   a water company

....

b)   domestic water users

....

Q3   Water is **treated** before it reaches our homes.

a)   Number the stages 1–4 to show the correct order of the processes in a **water treatment** plant.

☐ Sedimentation   ☐ Filtration through sand beds

☐ Chlorination   ☐ Filtration through a wire mesh

b)   Why are two filtration processes needed? ....

....

c)   Name a chemical used in the sedimentation process. ....

d)   Why are the purification processes unable to remove impurities such as ammonium nitrate?

....

e)   Why is chlorination used in the purification process?

....

Q4   Helen's house has an **old plumbing system**. She's concerned about **pollutants** in the tap water.

a)   What form of pollution in the tap water could be caused by the plumbing system?

....

b)   Helen's water supply comes from a reservoir located in an area of intensive agriculture.
Suggest **two** other forms of pollutant which could be present in the tap water.

....

Module C4 — Chemical Economics

Water Purity

Q5 **Sodium sulfate** reacts with **barium chloride** in a precipitation reaction.

a) What is a **precipitation reaction**?

....

b) Complete the word equation for this reaction.

sodium sulfate + barium chloride → barium .... + ...

c) Complete and balance the symbol equation for this reaction.

Na_2SO_4 + ... → .... + ...NaCl

HINT: The sulfate ion is SO_4^{2-} and the barium ion is Ba^{2+}.

Q6 Sam creates a flow chart as a key to help her identify **halide anions** present in a sample of water.

a) Finish the flow chart by completing the empty boxes.

White precipitate

Water sample → Add dilute nitric acid →

Br^- ions

I^- ions

b) Complete the following symbol equations involved in testing for halide ions.

i) $AgNO_3$ + KCl → .... + KNO_3

iii) Ag^+ + Br^- → ....

ii) .... + ... → AgI + $NaNO_3$

Q7 People in developing countries often can't get **clean water**.

a) How can drinking dirty water make you ill?

....

....

b) Suggest how developing countries can help ensure everyone has a supply of clean water.

....

....

Q8 Some countries get fresh water by **distilling** seawater.

a) Give **one** advantage of this method.

....

b) Give **two** disadvantages of this method.

....

....

Module C4 — Chemical Economics

Mixed Questions — Module C4

Q1   Three forms of the element carbon are shown in the diagram.

R   S   T

○ carbon atoms

a)   Identify the different forms by name.

R ....   S ....   T ....

b)   Form **R** has a melting point of 3652 °C. Form **S** has a melting point of 3550 °C.

i)   Explain why forms R and S have very high melting points.
You should mention structure and bonding in your answer.

....

....

ii)   Predict whether the melting point of form **T** will be greater than, the same as, or lower
than those of the other two forms. Justify your answer.

....

....

Q2   Orwell reacted silicon with chlorine to produce the liquid silicon chloride ($SiCl_4$).

a)   Calculate the **relative formula mass** of silicon chloride.

....

b)   Calculate the **percentage mass** of chlorine in silicon chloride.

....

c)   Write down the **balanced symbol equation** for the reaction.

....

d)   How much chlorine would Orwell need to react with **2.8 g of silicon**?

....

....

e)   Orwell predicted he would obtain 17.0 g of silicon chloride, however he only obtained 13.0 g.
Calculate the **percentage yield** for this reaction.

....

f)   Suggest two ways in which some of the product may have been lost from the reaction container.
(There was no filtration involved in the process.)

....

....

Mixed Questions — Module C4

Q3 The diagram shows the **pH scale**.

1	2	3	4	5	6	7	8	9	10	11	12	13

↑ black coffee   ↑ magnesium hydroxide

a) The pH values of black coffee and milk of magnesia are marked on the diagram.

   i) Is black coffee neutral, acidic or alkaline? ....

   ii) Is magnesium hydroxide neutral, acidic or alkaline? ....

b) Indigestion is caused by excess acid in the stomach. Magnesium hydroxide, $Mg(OH)_2$, is used in indigestion remedies. Explain how magnesium hydroxide can help with indigestion.

   ....

Q4 Some solid **magnesium oxide** was added to **HCl** solution in a test tube. The reactants and the products are shown, but the equation is **not** balanced.

$$MgO \ (s) \ + \ HCl \ (aq) \ \rightarrow \ D \ (aq) \ + \ H_2O \ (l)$$

a) **i)** Give the chemical formula of substance **D**. ....

   ii) What would be observed as the reaction **proceeded**?

   ....

b) When solid magnesium oxide was added to a substance **S**, magnesium sulfate and water were formed. Identify S by name or formula. ....

c) Describe a **chemical test** you could use to distinguish between a solution of magnesium sulfate and a solution of substance D.

   ....

   ....

Q5 **Detergents** are usually used in washing machines.

a) Indicate whether the following statements are **true** or **false**.

   True False

   i) Detergents are always more effective at high temperatures. ☐ ☐

   ii) Washing clothes at lower temperatures is more environmentally friendly. ☐ ☐

   iii) Most synthetic detergents are alkalis. ☐ ☐

   iv) The hydrophobic end of detergent molecules bonds to grease molecules. ☐ ☐

b) Explain why dry cleaning might remove a **paint stain** that a detergent failed to remove.

   ....

   ....

Mixed Questions — Module C4

Q6 The **cost** of producing ammonia in the Haber process depends on several factors.

a) Give **four factors** on which the cost of producing ammonia depends.

....

....

b) The temperature and pressure conditions for the Haber process could be described as **'a compromise'**. With reference to these conditions explain what the 'compromise' is.

....

....

....

c) Suggest two reasons why ammonia is made using **continuous production** rather than batch production.

....

....

Q7 **Fertilisers** dramatically increase the quantity and quality of crops.

a) Ammonium nitrate is a good fertiliser, because it contains two sources of nitrogen.

i) Write a balanced equation to show the reaction of ammonia (NH_3) with nitric acid (HNO_3) to produce ammonium nitrate (NH_4NO_3).

....

ii) This a neutralisation reaction. Explain why.

....

iii) Why is nitrogen important to plants?

....

b) Explain how excess fertiliser on fields can kill fish in local rivers.

....

....

Q8 Explain why the following substances are added in the **water purification** process:

a) aluminium sulfate ....

....

b) chlorine gas ....

Static Electricity

Q1   **Circle** the pairs of charges that would attract each other and **underline** those that would repel.

positive and positive   positive and negative   negative and positive   negative and negative

Q2   Fill in the gaps in these sentences with the words below.

electrons	positive	static	friction	insulating	negative

.... electricity can build up when two .... materials are rubbed together. The .... moves .... from one material onto the other. This leaves a .... charge on one of the materials and a .... charge on the other.

Q3   The sentences below are wrong. Write out a **correct** version for each.

a)   A polythene rod becomes negatively charged when rubbed with a duster because it loses electrons.

....

....

b)   A charged polythene rod will repel small pieces of paper if they are placed near it.

....

....

c)   The closer two charged objects are together, the less strongly they attract or repel.

....

....

d)   If a positively charged object is connected to earth by a metal strap, electrons flow through the strap from the object to the ground, and the object is safely discharged.

....

....

e)   Build-up of static can cause sparks if the distance between the object and the earth is big enough.

....

....

Static Electricity

Q4 A library had to be closed after nylon carpets were fitted. People complained of electric shocks when they touched the metal handrail on the stairs. Explain why they were experiencing shocks.

....

....

Q5 Russell hates his blue jumper. Whenever he takes it off his hair stands on end. Explain why this happens.

....

....

Q6 Choose from the words below to complete the passage.

fuel   explosion   metal   paper rollers   wood   grain chutes   sparks   earthing   plastic

Static electricity can be dangerous when refuelling cars. If too much static builds up, there

might be .... which could set fire to the ....

This could lead to an .... To prevent this happening, the nozzle is

made of .... so the charge is conducted away. There are similar safety

problems with .... and ....

Q7 As Peter switched off his TV, he noticed that the screen was dusty. When he wiped it with his finger he heard a **crackling** sound and felt a slight **electric shock**.

Peter made two statements about what happened. Give a **reason** why he said each of the following:

a) *"The screen must have been at a high voltage."*

....

....

b) *"When I touched it, part of the screen was discharged to earth."*

....

....

Q8 Explain why **anti-static** sprays are sometimes used in hospital operating theatres.

....

....

Uses of Static Electricity

Q1   The diagram shows an electrostatic paint sprayer.

  a)   How do the drops of paint become charged?

  ....

  b)   Why does this help produce a fine spray?

  ....

  c)   Explain how the paint drops are attracted to the object being sprayed.

  ....

  d)   Explain why the object being painted doesn't need to be turned round while it is being sprayed.

  ....

Q2   Complete this paragraph by choosing words from the list below.

precipitator	negative	plates	charge	particles	positive	heavy
	attracted	fall off	electron	compressed		

  Smoke contains tiny .... The smoke can be cleaned up with a dust

  ....

  One sort uses a wire grid with a high negative .... to give the particles a

  negative charge. They then pass between two metal .... which have

  a .... charge.

  The particles are .... to the plates. The particles clump together

  and when they are .... enough, they ....

Q3   A defibrillator is a machine used by emergency medical staff to give electric shocks.

  a)   When are defibrillators used and why?

  ....

  b)   How is the electricity transferred to the patient?

  ....

  c)   Explain what safety precautions are taken when using a defibrillator and why.

  ....

  ....

Charge in Circuits

Q1 Use the words below to complete the passage.
You may need to use some words more than once.

protons	electrons	resistance	voltage	increase	reduce

Current is the flow of .... around a circuit. Current flows through a

component which has a .... across it. Resistance tends to

.... the flow. To increase the current in a circuit you can

.... the resistance or .... the voltage.

Q2 Connect the quantities with their units.

 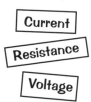 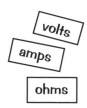

Q3 The flow of electricity in circuits can be compared to the flow of water in pipes.

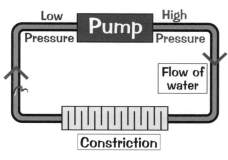

a) In a water 'circuit', what is the equivalent to electrical **current**?

....

b) If there is a water pump in the system,
what electrical device does it correspond to?

....

c) What corresponds to electrical **resistance** in a water 'circuit'?

....

d) The pump is turned up. What would the equivalent action be in an electrical circuit?

....

Q4 A current flows around an electrical circuit.

a) If the circuit is broken, what happens to the current?

....

b) Give an example of a safety feature designed to break a circuit.

....

Top Tips: The current is the flow of electrons which are pushed around a circuit by the voltage. The greater the voltage, the more current flows. Anything that slows the flow of electrons down is a resistor. Slowing the electrons decreases the current. Make sure you get the hang of this and you'll be scooping up the marks like a small child let loose at the pick and mix counter. Enjoy.

Fuses and Safe Plugs

Q1 Answer the following questions about **electric plugs**:

a) Why is the body of a plug made of rubber or plastic?

....

b) Explain why some parts of a plug are made from copper or brass.

....

c) What material is the cable insulation made from, and why?

....

Q2 Use the words below to complete these rules for wiring a plug.

outer   bare   live   earth   neutral   insulation   firmly   green and yellow

a) Strip the .... off the end of each wire.

b) Connect the brown wire to the .... terminal.

c) Connect the blue wire to the .... terminal.

d) Connect the .... wire to the .... terminal.

e) Check all the wires are .... screwed in with no .... bits showing.

f) The cable grip must be securely fastened over the .... covering of the cable.

Q3 This plug is **incorrectly** wired. Write down the **three** mistakes.

1. ....

2. ....

3. ....

= Neutral
= Live
= Earth

Q4 Put these events in the correct order to describe what happens when a fault occurs in an earthed kettle. Label the events from 1 to 4.

☐ The device is isolated from the live wire.

☐ A big current flows out through the earth wire.

☐ A big surge in current blows the fuse.

☐ A fault allows the live wire to touch the metal case.

Q5 A '**double insulated**' hairdryer uses a current of 0.25 A.

a) Andrea has fuses rated 0.25 A, 2 A and 8 A.
Which fuse should she fit in the plug for the hairdryer? ....

b) Why does the hairdryer **not** need an **earth wire**?

....

Resistance

Q1 Indicate whether these statements are **true** or **false**.

True False

Current flows from positive to negative. ☐ ☐

An ammeter should be connected in parallel with a component. ☐ ☐

Items that are in series can be in any order. ☐ ☐

A voltmeter should be connected in series with a component. ☐ ☐

Q2 Complete these sentences by circling the correct word from each pair.

a) Increasing the voltage **increases** / **decreases** the current that flows.

b) If the p.d. is kept constant, to increase the current you need to **increase** / **decrease** the resistance.

c) If the resistance is increased, **more** / **less** current will flow if the p.d. is kept constant.

Q3 Fabio sets up a standard circuit using a **variable resistor** to test the resistance of a material.

a) Label the standard test circuit components using the words in the box below.

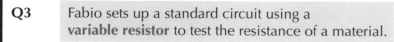

| voltmeter | material |
| variable resistor | ammeter |

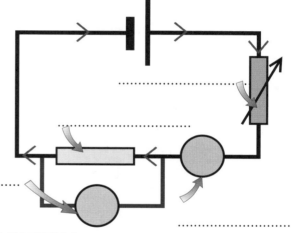

b) Fabio sets the variable resistor at zero resistance. He measures a current of 2.4 A and a p.d. of 6 V. Calculate the resistance of the material.

....

c) How would Fabio use the variable resistor to help get a reliable result from his experiment?

....

Q4 Fill in the missing values in the table below.

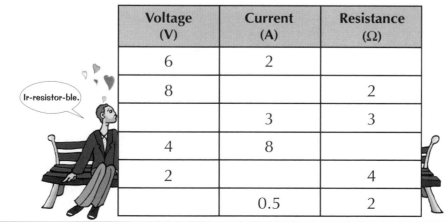

Ir-resistor-ble.

Voltage (V)	Current (A)	Resistance (Ω)
6	2	
8		2
	3	3
4	8	
2		4
	0.5	2

Ultrasound Scans and Treatment

Q1 Sound waves are **longitudinal** waves.

a) Describe the difference between **longitudinal** and **transverse** waves.

....

....

b) What is meant by the **frequency** of a wave?

....

c) When sound waves travel through a material they produce **compressions** and **rarefactions**. What do these words mean?

....

....

Q2 An oscilloscope (CRO) can be used to show a sound wave as a **transverse** wave.

a) Mark the **wavelength** and the **amplitude** of the wave on the diagram.

b) **i)** What does the **amplitude** of a wave tell you?

....

....

ii) If a sound wave has a small amplitude, will it sound loud or quiet? ....

Q3 A concentrated beam of **ultrasound** can be used to treat kidney stones.

a) What is ultrasound?

....

b) What effect does the ultrasound beam have on kidney stones?

....

c) How are the kidney stone remains removed from the body?

....

d) Give two reasons why using ultrasound is a good way of treating kidney stones.

1. ....

2. ....

Module P4 — Radiation for Life

Ultrasound Scans and Treatment

Q4   Ultrasound can be used to monitor the growth of a foetus.

a)   Complete the following using words from the list.

foetus	reflected	media	detected	echoes	body	image

Ultrasound waves can pass through most parts of the ....

Whenever an ultrasound wave reaches the boundary between two different

................................, some of the wave is .... back and can be

.... These .... can be processed by a computer

to give an .... of the ....

b)   Give one other use of ultrasound in medicine, apart from
prenatal scanning and kidney stone treatment.

....

Q5   Indicate whether the following statements are **true** or **false**.

	True	False
Ultrasound waves have frequencies greater than 20 000 Hz.	☐	☐
X-rays are used for prenatal scanning.	☐	☐
Ultrasound can cause cancer if a patient is exposed to a high dose.	☐	☐
X-rays travel easily through soft tissue.	☐	☐
Ultrasound and X-rays are both good ways of looking at broken bones in the body.	☐	☐

Q6   Ultrasound can be used in a similar way to **X-rays**.

a)   Why is ultrasound safer than X-rays?

....

b)   State whether X-rays or ultrasound would be used to
investigate a suspected broken bone, and explain why.

....

....

Top Tips: Amazing really that you can learn so much using sound waves. The main thing
to remember is that ultrasound is safe and extremely useful. You might be asked to explain **how**
ultrasound is used in prenatal scans and for removing kidney stones — so make sure you know.

Ionising Radiation

Q1 X-rays and gamma rays are electromagnetic waves.

a) Describe how gamma rays are released.

....

b) How are X-rays produced?

....

c) Which of the two is easier to control? Explain your answer.

....

Q2 Use the words in the list below to complete the paragraph.

ionisation	nuclear	molecules	cells	cancer	destroy

When X-ray and .... radiation enter .... in the body

they may collide with .... and cause .... Fairly low

doses of radiation can cause .... — creating mutant cells which

multiply uncontrollably. Higher doses can .... cells completely.

Q3 The three different types of nuclear radiation can all be dangerous.

a) Which **two** types of radiation can pass into the human body
from outside? Circle the correct answers.

alpha   beta   gamma

b) i) Which type of radiation is usually most dangerous if it's inhaled or swallowed? ....

ii) Describe the effects this type of radiation can have on the human body.

....

....

Q4 When radiographers take X-ray 'photographs' or scans of patients, they themselves are exposed to X-rays. Write down two precautions radiographers can take to minimise their exposure to X-rays.

1. ....

2. ....

Radioactive Decay

Q1 Write down the atomic number and mass number for each type of radiation.

a) alpha   atomic number = ... 　　　mass number = ...

b) beta   atomic number = ... 　　　mass number = ...

c) gamma   atomic number = ... 　　　mass number = ...

Q2 Complete the passage using words from the list.

chemical   random   decay   radiation   nucleus   element   temperature

Radioactive .... is a totally .... process.

At some point an unstable .... will decay and emit

.... What is left behind is often a new ....

There is nothing that can make an unstable nucleus decay. It is unaffected by

.... or .... bonding.

Q3 Complete the table below by choosing the correct word from each column.

Radiation Type	Ionising power weak/moderate/ strong	Charge positive/none/ negative	Relative mass no mass/ small/large	Penetrating power low/moderate/ high	Relative speed slow/fast/ very fast
alpha					
beta					
gamma					

Q4 When a nucleus emits an alpha or beta particle, the nucleus changes.

a) What happens to a nucleus when it emits an **alpha particle**?

....

....

....

b) What happens to a nucleus when it emits a **beta particle**?

....

....

Module P4 — Radiation for Life

Radioactive Decay

Q5 Explain clearly why:

a) an alpha particle is written as ^4_2He or $^4_2\alpha$.

....

b) a radium atom $^{226}_{88}\text{Ra}$ turns into a radon atom $^{222}_{86}\text{Rn}$ when it emits an alpha particle.

....

c) a beta particle is written as $^0_{-1}\text{e}$ or $^0_{-1}\beta$.

....

d) a carbon-14 atom $^{14}_6\text{C}$ turns into a nitrogen atom $^{14}_7\text{N}$ when it emits a beta particle.

....

Q6 The diagram shows uranium-238 decaying into thorium by alpha and gamma emission.

$$^{238}_{92}\text{U} \longrightarrow \text{He} \quad \text{Th} \quad \gamma$$

a) What effect does the **gamma ray** emission have on the uranium nucleus?

....

b) Write the full nuclear equation for this decay, clearly showing the atomic and mass numbers.

....

Q7 When radioactive decay occurs, α, β or γ radiation is emitted and new elements may be formed.

a) Write a nuclear equation to show thorium-234, $^{234}_{90}\text{Th}$, decaying to form protactinium, $^{234}_{91}\text{Pa}$.

....

b) Write a nuclear equation to show radon, $^{222}_{86}\text{Rn}$, decaying by **alpha** emission.

....

Top Tips: Put 'nuclear' in front of anything and it sounds extra scary*. Fortunately, nuclear **equations** aren't nearly as scary as they sound. Learn the atomic numbers and mass numbers for each type of radiation and you'll be well on the way to equation bliss. After a bit of practice you'll find that balancing the equations isn't that bad — just a bit of adding and subtracting. *except the word **sheep**

Radioactivity and Half-Life

Q1   Complete the passage using some of the words given below.

> long   photo   time   all   half   ionise   atoms   gamma   alpha
> beta   short   increases   decreases   decay

The radioactivity of a sample always .... over time. Each time a decay

happens ...., ... or .... radiation is emitted.

The half-life is the .... taken for .... of the unstable

.... now present to .... An isotope with a ....

half-life decays more quickly than an isotope with a .... half-life.

Q2   The graph shows how the count rate of a radioactive isotope declines with time.

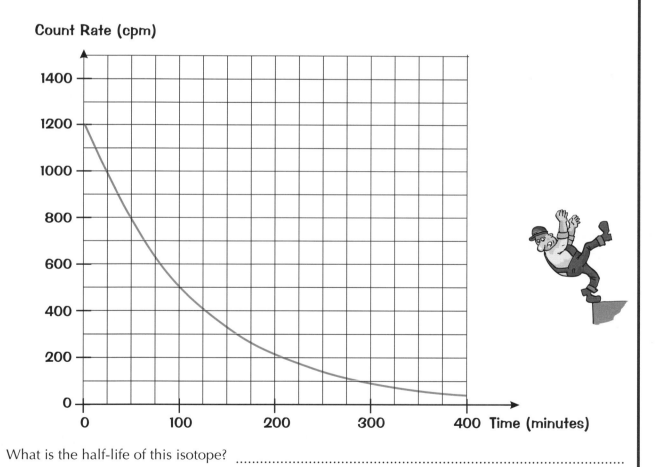

Count Rate (cpm)

a)   What is the half-life of this isotope? ....

b)   What was the count rate after 3 half-lives? ....

c)   What fraction of the original radioactive nuclei will still be unstable after 5 half-lives?

....

d)   After how long was the count rate down to 100? ....

Radioactivity and Half-Life

Q3 The activity of a radioisotope is 960 cpm. 1 hour later, the activity has dropped to 15 cpm. What is the source's half-life? Tick the correct box.

☐ 15 mins   ☐ 10 mins   ☐ 12 mins   ☐ 3 mins

Q4 The half-life of uranium-238 is 4500 million years. The half-life of carbon-14 is 5730 years.

a) What do the '238' in "uranium-238" and the '14' in "carbon-14" mean?

....

....

b) If you start with a sample of each element and the two samples have equal activity, which will lose its radioactivity more quickly? Circle the correct answer.

uranium-238   carbon-14

Q5 A radioactive isotope has a half-life of 40 seconds.

You'll need to change 6 minutes into seconds.

a) What fraction of the original unstable nuclei will still be present after 6 minutes?

....

....

b) **i)** If the initial count rate of the sample was 8000 counts per minute, what would be the approximate count rate after 6 minutes?

....

....

ii) After how many whole **minutes** would the count rate have fallen below 10 counts per minute?

....

....

Q6 Nick was trying to explain half-life to his little brother. He said, "isotopes with a long half-life are always more dangerous than those with a short half-life."

Is Nick right? Explain your answer.

....

....

....

Background Radiation

Q1 Which of the following are **true**? Circle the appropriate letters.

    A About half of the UK's background radiation comes from radon gas.

    B The nuclear industry is responsible for about 10% of background radiation in the UK.

    C If there were no radioactive substances on Earth, there would be no background radiation.

Q2 The level of background radiation varies from place to place. For each of the following, indicate whether the background level will be **higher** or **lower** than average and explain your answer.

    a) In a plane at high altitude, the level will be **higher** / **lower** than average because:

    ....

    b) In a mine, the level will usually be **higher** / **lower** than average because:

    ....

    c) In houses built above granite rocks, the level will usually be **higher** / **lower** than average because:

    ....

Q3 Peter did an experiment to compare equal quantities of two radioactive materials. Here are his results and conclusion.

Material tested	Radiation measured (counts per second)
None	50
Material A	200
Material B	400

CONCLUSION
"Both materials are radioactive. Material B is twice as radioactive as Material A."

Is Peter's conclusion correct? Give a reason for your answer.

....

....

Q4 The concentration of **radon** gas found in people's homes varies across the UK.

    a) Why does the concentration vary across the country?

    ....

    b) Explain why high concentrations of radon are dangerous.

    ....

    c) How can people in high radon areas reduce the radon concentration in their homes?

    ....

148

Medical Uses of Radiation

Q1 Complete the following paragraph on radiotherapy using the words provided.

ill centre normal kill cells focused cancer rotating radiotherapy

High doses of gamma radiation will .... living ....

Because of this, gamma radiation is used to treat .... This is called

....

Gamma rays are .... on the tumour using a wide beam. Damage to

.... cells can make the patient feel very .... This damage

is minimised by .... the radioactive source around the body, keeping the

tumour at the ....

Q2 Iodine-131 is commonly used as a tracer in medicine.

a) Normal iodine has a mass number of 127. Why is it no good as a tracer?

....

b) The thyroid gland normally absorbs iodine.
Describe how iodine-131 can be used to detect if the thyroid gland is working properly.

....

....

....

....

Q3 The table shows the properties of four radioisotopes.

a) Which radioisotope would be best to use as a medical tracer and why?

....

....

....

Radioisotope	Half-life	Type of emission
technetium-99	6 hours	beta/gamma
phosphorus-32	14 days	beta
cobalt-60	5 years	beta/gamma

b) Which radioisotope would a hospital use to treat cancer patients? Explain your answer.

....

....

Module P4 — Radiation for Life

Medical Uses of Radiation

Q4 The diagram shows how radiation can be used to sterilise surgical instruments.

radioactive source

thick lead

a) What kind of radioactive source is used, and why? In your answer, mention the **type** of radiation emitted (α, β or γ) and the **half-life** of the source.

....

....

....

b) What is the purpose of the thick lead?

....

c) Similar machines can be used to treat fruit before it is exported from South America to Europe, to stop it going bad on the long journey. How does irradiating the fruit help?

....

....

Q5 A patient has a radioactive source injected into her body to test her kidneys.

A healthy kidney will get rid of the radioactive material quickly (to the bladder). Damaged kidneys take longer to do this.

The results of the test, for both the patient's kidneys, are shown opposite.

Kidney A

Count Rate

Time

Kidney B

Count Rate

Time

a) Explain how the doctor knew which kidney was working well and which was not.

....

....

b) Explain why an alpha source would **not** be suitable for this investigation.

....

....

Top Tips: There's no doubt about it — this is physics being obviously, genuinely **useful** — and radiation being Mr Nice Guy. Anyway, make sure you know **why** each type of radiation is used in each situation — and remember that you **never** want an alpha source inside the body.
Final tip: saying "radioisotope" three times every day for a year can increase your IQ by 20 points.

Non-Medical Uses of Radiation

Q1 The table shows some commonly used radioisotopes and the type of radiation they emit.

a) Which of these isotopes would be most suitable for these applications?

i) A smoke detector

....

ii) To sterilise pre-packed food

....

Radioisotope	Decays by...
strontium-90	beta emission
americium-241	mainly alpha emission
cobalt-60	beta and gamma emission

iii) To measure the thickness of paper as it is being manufactured

....

b) What further information about these isotopes would you want before you considered using them?

....

Q2 Carbon-14 makes up 1/10 000 000 of the carbon in the air.

a) Name one gas in the air which contains carbon.

....

b) What proportion of the carbon present in organisms alive now is carbon-14?

....

c) What happens to the level of carbon-14 in a plant or animal after it dies?

....

Q3 The following sentences explain how a smoke detector works, but they are in the wrong order.

Put them in order by labelling them 1 (first) to 6 (last).

[ ] The circuit is broken so no current flows.

[1] The radioactive source emits alpha particles.

[ ] A current flows between the electrodes — the alarm stays off.

[ ] The alarm sounds.

[ ] The air between the electrodes is ionised by the alpha particles.

[ ] A fire starts and smoke particles absorb the alpha radiation.

Non-Medical Uses of Radiation

Q4   Eviloilco knows that its oil pipeline is leaking somewhere between points A and B.

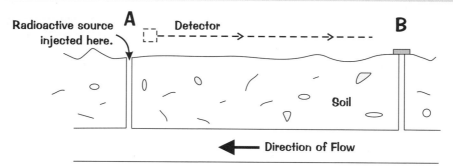

This is how Eviloilco plans to find the leak.

> We will inject a source of alpha radiation into the pipeline at point A. (This source has a long half-life — giving us better value for money in the long term.) After injecting the radioactive material, we will pass a sensor along the surface above the pipeline — and so detect where radiation is escaping, hence pinpointing the leak.

a)   Give **two** reasons why Eviloilco has made a bad choice of radioactive source, and describe the type of source they should use.

....

....

....

b)   Even if they use the correct type of radioactive source, their plan will still fail. Why?

....

Q5   A wooden spoon from an archaeological dig was found to have 1 part C-14 to 80 000 000 parts carbon. Work out when the wood was **living material**. (The half-life of C-14 is 5730 years.)

....

Q6   Uranium-238 has a half-life of 4.5 billion years.

Rock, 243 019 yrs, but young at heart. Cumbria based, GSOH. Likes: the outdoors. Dislikes: dogs, moss

Mal 45, seek curv foot mor

a)   Explain how the decay of uranium can be used to date rocks.

....

....

b)   The Earth is around 4.5 billion years old. How much of the Earth's original uranium-238 is left?

....

c)   A meteorite contains uranium-238 and lead in a ratio of 1:3. How old is the meteorite?

....

Nuclear Power

Q1 Choose from the following words to complete the passage.

split	chemical	turbine	electricity	uranium	water	wine
	steam	moped	generator	reactors	heat	

Inside a nuclear reactor, ... or plutonium atoms

.... and release .... energy. This

energy is used to turn .... into ....

The steam then turns a ...., which in turn drives a

.............................., producing ....

Q2 In a nuclear reactor a controlled fission **chain reaction** takes place.

a) Describe a fission **chain reaction**, starting with
a single uranium nucleus absorbing a **slow-moving neutron**.

....

....

....

....

b) Write a nuclear equation for an atom of uranium-235 absorbing a neutron.

....

Q3 Nuclear reactors have **control rods**, which are usually made of boron.

a) How do these boron rods control the reaction?

....

b) What would happen if there were **no** control rods (or other control mechanism) in the reactor?

....

c) What would happen if there were **too many** control rods in the reactor?

....

Nuclear Power

Q4 The diagram shows a gas-cooled nuclear reactor.

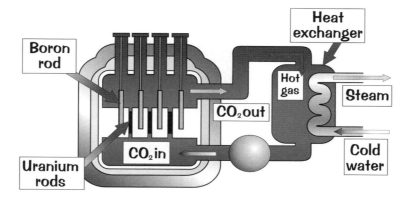

a) Why are neutrons injected into the reactor when it is started up?

....

b) Describe how heat is generated in the reactor.

....

....

c) What is the function of the carbon dioxide?

....

d) Why is the reactor surrounded with a very thick layer of concrete?

....

Q5 Uranium-236 is an unstable isotope of uranium.

a) Describe how uranium-236 is formed inside a nuclear reactor.

....

b) U-236 decays to form two neutrons and two new elements: krypton-90 and barium-144. Write the nuclear equation for this decay. (Atomic masses Kr = 36, Ba = 56, U = 92.)

....

Top Tips: The key thing with nuclear power is to remember what goes on in the reactor. It's really just one big nuclear kettle. A controlled chain reaction is set up and releases heat, which is used to heat water and produce steam. After that it's just like almost all power stations — the steam turns a turbine which turns a generator which makes electricity, which makes cups of tea galore.

Mixed Questions — Module P4

Q1 The diagram shows an aircraft being refuelled. No safety precautions have been taken.

a) **i)** Explain how static electricity could cause an explosion in this situation.

....

....

ii) Give one precaution that can be taken to avoid this danger.

....

b) The aircraft needs a new lick of paint. Describe how static electricity could be used to make sure that an even coat of paint is sprayed onto the aircraft.

....

....

Q2 Radioactive tracers are important in medicine and industry.

a) Explain what is meant by the word 'tracer'.

....

b) Give two reasons why an alpha source would not be suitable to use as a **medical** tracer.

....

....

c) Give one example of how tracers are used in industry.

....

Q3 The diagram below shows part of a chain reaction.

a) What is the name of the type of radioactive decay shown in the diagram? ....

b) This decay happens as part of a chain reaction. Describe what happens in this chain reaction.

....

....

Mixed Questions — Module P4

Q4 Approximately one in 10 000 000 of the carbon molecules found in living plants or animals are atoms of the radioactive isotope carbon-14. After a plant or animal dies this proportion starts to decrease. Carbon-14 has a half-life of 5730 years.

a) Calculate the fraction of the atoms in a pure sample of carbon-14 that will still not have decayed after 10 half-lives have gone by.

....

....

b) Approximately how old is a bone fragment in which the proportion of carbon-14 is one part in 50 000 000? Explain your answer.

....

....

....

c) Suggest why carbon dating is unreliable for samples more than about 50 000 years old.

....

....

Q5 Paul wants to set the mood for his date with some romantic lighting. He dims the lights using a dimmer switch which works as a variable resistor.

I can still see your face...

a) Describe how the dimmer switch dims the lights.

....

....

Position	Resistance	Current
1	50	
2		2.3
3		9.2

b) Because he's such a charmer, Paul entertains his date by taking some current and resistance readings with the dimmer switch in three different positions. The voltage is 230 V. Complete the table.

c) In which position will the lights be brightest? ....

Q6 Ultra sound and X-rays are both used in medicine.

a) Explain how ultrasound is used in prenatal scans.

....

....

b) Why would you not use X-rays for this type of scan?

....

Mixed Questions — Module P4

Q7 Modern electrical appliances are carefully designed to prevent the user getting an electric shock.

a) Tom's washing machine develops a fault. Part of the live wire touches the metal case.
Explain how the earth wire and fuse work together to prevent Tom getting an electric shock.

....

....

b) Bob buys a new 'double insulated' television set.

i) Which wires are in the plug? ....

ii) What is meant by 'double insulated'?

....

Q8 Fay measures the count rate of a sample of pure copper-64 in her home, using a Geiger counter. The graph below shows her results.

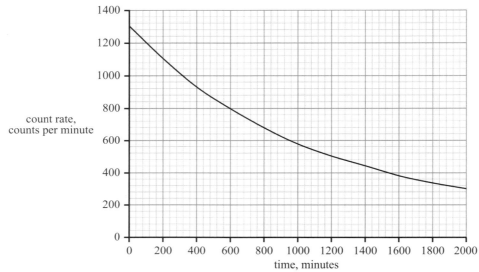

a) Fay had previously measured the background rate to be 100 counts per minute.
Find the half-life of copper-64.

....

b) She takes her Geiger counter to her friend's house and finds the background rate is much higher.
Give one reason why background radiation changes from place to place?

....

c) Her friend explains that she lives in a high **radon** area.

i) What disease is her friend more at risk of developing? ....

ii) How could she reduce the concentration of radon in her house?

....

Module P4 — Radiation for Life

SCHW41